ELBOWS UP!

ELBOWS

UP!

Canadian Voices of Resilience and Resistance

Edited by
ELAMIN ABDELMAHMOUD

McCLELLAND & STEWART

Contents

ELBOWS UP!

AN INVITATION TO CONTRIBUTE TO AN IMPORTANT NEW BOOK

Working Title: "The New Romans"

Subject: What some well known Canadians really think of Americans
and the U.S.

Editor: A.W. Purdy

Publisher: M.G. Hurtig

Payment: $20.00 for poetry (about 40 lines - slightly more or less)
or $20.00 for prose (about 1,000 words). Contributions
must not have been previously published in book form.

Format: About 60 pages of prose and 30 pages of poetry, about 40
contributing Canadian poets, writers, broadcasters, critics,
politicians, political scientists, philosophers, etc.

Contributions: To be sent to A.W. Purdy, R.R. #1, Ameliasburg,
Ontario.

Deadline: September 1, 1967

About The Book: Many Canadians feel the overpowering effect of
the U.S.A. is not in the best interest of Canada. This book is
meant to explore the aspects of American culture, social values
and morality that the authors find objectionable and even dangerous. Here is an excellent opportunity to speak out on a subject
most often ignored by Canada's press. Bear in mind, we're not
necessarily talking about business or economics. What we'd like
to have from contributors to this book is strong, outspoken and
honest comment on such things as the reality of "The American
Dream," the commonplace violence in American society, the virt-
ually accepted Governmental "credibility gap," the resurgence of
McCarthyism in the U.S., American involvement in Vietnam, the C.I.A.
and American intervention abroad, the export of American "culture"
as exemplified by U.S. television, "democracy" and "freedom"
defined in terms of napalm, Watts or non-violent protest -
The John Birch Society, murder, and "the right to bear arms," etc.

Will the book be anti-American? Definitely!

Just to stir up controversy? Definitely not! This book will be
highly controversial, and will likely be the subject of much
criticism. Most of all we hope the book to represent an honest
expression, by respected Canadians of facets of American society
many Canadians do not accept.

The editor and publisher believe that in swallowing-
whole American values, American publications, movies and television,
there is some danger of Canadian indigestion. We also believe
that Americans and Canadians are not identical as to thinking and
beliefs, and that we might even have more in common with Quebec
than the U.S. We accept the idea that Canadians also live in a
glass house, but believe we have the right to throw stones in any
direction we like, especially southward. "None of us are perfect,
but some of us are less perfect." (Confucius)

We are not ultra nationalists, just ordinary ones, and
believe that Canada as a country still has much to lose during the
next hundred years (like self-respect) if we can't stand up on our
hind legs and say what we think. We hope you'll be a contributor to
this book, and that payment will be least of the incentives.

"Al Purdy"

ELAMIN ABDELMAHMOUD

Introduction:
The Sturdiness of an
Unfinished Project

If Expo 67 in Montreal was the loud, chatty corner of Canada's 100th birthday party in 1967, Edmonton's Second Century Week was the quiet, intellectual circle. Students from more than fifty universities and colleges travelled across the country, pouring into Edmonton to reflect on the meaning of Canada. There were lectures and debates, there were literary salons, and there was, of course, folk music. At one of the folk music parties, amid the singalongs and the chatter about what Canada's next 100 years might look like, the legendary publisher and activist Mel Hurtig and the prolific poet Al Purdy were huddled, conspiring.

Purdy griped to Hurtig about the way the United States treats Canada. And who could blame him? Purdy spent his career as something of an unofficial poet laureate of a nation reluctant to speak for itself, more than happy to defer to stories told by its neighbour. Purdy wanted to assemble Canadian opinions of the U.S. as a book. Hurtig listened. Three hours later, Hurtig says in his memoir, the pair was set on making the book a reality. They settled on the title *The New Romans*.

Purdy and Hurtig co-authored a fiery invitation to coax Canada's literary luminaries into the project. "The editor and author believe that in swallowing-whole American values, American publications, movies and television, there is some danger of Canadian indigestion," they wrote, indignant about the amount of space the U.S. takes up in the Canadian imagination. They were by no means intense nationalists, they told invitees, but this was no time to be timid—they "believe that Canada as a country still has much to lose during the next hundred years (like self-respect) if we can't stand up on our hind legs and say what we think." They had a hunch that this was a conversation that Canadians desperately needed.

Even before publication, Hurtig positioned the book as the exhale the country was looking for. He promised controversy and impolite talk, and he had the country's literary heavyweights on his side—Mordecai Richler, Margaret Atwood, Margaret Laurence, and Farley Mowat were among the lot who had answered the call. Hurtig had bookmarks printed advertising *The New Romans*, calling it "one of the most controversial books ever published in Canada." The subtitle was short and to the point: "Candid Canadian Opinions of the U.S."

As it turns out, their hunch was right. By July of 1968, two months before publication, *The New Romans* had already amassed an astonishing 20,000 advance orders. Here was a country at a turning point, ravenous for a window into itself.

Nearly sixty years later, as luck would have it, Mel Hurtig's daughter Leslie, who runs the Vancouver Writers Festival, and McClelland & Stewart publisher Stephanie Sinclair were huddled, conspiring. The occasion hadn't even changed much: the shadow of the United States had once again unsettled a quiet anxiety. Only this time, the threat was no longer implied. From the Oval Office, an American president repeatedly vowed to make Canada the 51st state; he called the sitting prime minister a "governor" to provoke a response. The book you're holding now began with Hurtig and Sinclair both recognizing that this is our moment to stand on our hind legs and say what we think. So, what do we have to say?

Elbows Up! is on the whole, admittedly, more combative than *The New Romans*. What is in the pages to come will be measured contemplation, yes, but there will also be anger, hurt, betrayal, and frustration spilling out. As I spent time with these contributions, I wondered if we have become more combative in the intervening fifty-seven years. Or is it more likely the prodigious talent of the offending American president to draw out an intense response?

But then again, perhaps it has been too long since Canada considered some existential questions. That wasn't the case fifty-seven years ago. Al Purdy and the gang had momentum on their side in 1968. *The New Romans* emerged in the middle of a rich era of Canada asking itself questions. Consider this: In 1965, the same year that Canada launched its new national flag, George Grant published his radical *Lament for a Nation*. Grant was dramatic in his framing—he subtitled it

"The Defeat of Canadian Nationalism"—so perhaps he did not anticipate the delightful irony that his book would launch a kind of renaissance of Canadian identity contemplation. Expo 67 followed a couple of years later, showcasing the country to the world just as Canada turned 100.

This was fertile soil for *The New Romans* to arrive in. It also meant Purdy's slate had the space of contemplation without the hanging threat of annexation in the air. Purdy and Hurtig's invitation may have been fiery, but the contributions exhibited a range in tones. Indeed, Richler turned the invitation to reflect on the U.S. into a mirror, picking up on Canada's "increasingly truculent, occasionally touching national pursuit of something or other we can be true to. A heritage. A tradition. *Anything.*"

We don't have such luxury of cool distance from the hovering danger, and the *Elbows Up!* contributions reflect that. These essays are teeming with urgency and movement. Carol Off writes that she has become convinced that "Canada didn't need an identity, it needed a shrink." Omar El Akkad takes on the "many deranged currents in which the United States is presently caught," while Jesse Wente warns from experience: "The new colonizer will seek to kill all the buffalo, whatever form that takes today."

Peter Mansbridge wonders where our newfound anger will take us, an anger he has never seen before. Speaking of anger, "An elbow is a weapon," writes Ann-Marie MacDonald. Some of that anger turns inwards, as Jay Baruchel rightly admonishes us for neglecting the advancement of our own stories in favour of American culture.

Still, the parallels between *The New Romans* and *Elbows Up!* are occasionally amusing. I was watching Justin Trudeau proclaim that "there isn't a snowball's chance in hell that Canada would become part of the United States" while reading Farley Mowat invert that exact sentiment in *The New Romans*: "I can no longer convince myself that we have even a snowball's chance in hell of escaping ultimate ravishment at the hands of the Yankee succubus," he writes. Mowat's contains the serenity of a man who knows he cannot win a fight; Trudeau's carries the hallmarks of a fight-or-flight response.

It's also not lost on me that in the very act of bringing this book to life, we are contributing to what Richler calls "one of the few original Canadian enterprises, the What-Is-Our-Identity business." But what would he have us do? Roll over? You can decide for yourself, as we have reprinted some of the most piercing pieces from *The New Romans* here.

Elbows Up!, then, is a work of necessity, a book that emerges out of multiple crises converging. It represents a collection of voices from across the country who have answered the call in an impossibly short timeframe, eager to enter a conversation that the country needs right now.

These contributions buck and protest under a recognition of an ordering reality: regardless of the political weather of the United States, our relationship with them cannot just be severed. Geography demands this, and industry backs up that demand. But what you will get from these pages is a sense of broadening possibility: that this relationship can be reconfigured, maybe even nudged out of the centre of Canada's cultural imagination. Even if the U.S. were to elect another Manifest

Destiny president, perhaps Canada could learn not to voluntarily hand over the country's sense of itself.

Yet the works in this book also buck and protest under a coursing defeatism that sometimes rears its head in Canadian culture. I cannot convey how quickly my enthusiasm dimmed as I flipped the pages of *The New Romans*, surprised by how so many of our literary heroes assumed it was inevitable that Canada would become subsumed by the United States, either economically, culturally, or literally.

"A good definition of Canada," Margaret Atwood once wrote, "might be that it is the only country that is being told repeatedly—from both inside and outside itself—that it doesn't really exist." At least for now, the voices from inside have quieted. Perhaps they're looking around, perhaps for the first time, and taking in what they can see, and for once, letting it add up to a country.

At the height of the annexation threats, when the "51st state" rhetoric was nearly daily, I met with a group of up-and-coming Indigenous journalists, all of them women, all in their twenties. Our conversation drifted to the news cycle and the group traded jokes about how disorienting it was to hear the word "sovereignty" so often at the heart of a national conversation—up until now, they said, they'd only heard sovereignty talked about by older Indigenous adults. "It's so crazy to see white people taking our word," one said, and the room exploded in laughter.

There is something instructive here: how might Canada understand itself differently if more Canadians understood that these recent threats do not constitute a new kind of encroachment on the self-determination of people who live here, but rather a continuation of the old encroachments?

Elbows Up! was built with this frame at its centre. Where Purdy and Hurtig were provocative, Sinclair and I began our invitation letter by urging contributors not to lose sight of the fact that not everyone watching the news will be surprised by the realization that treaties can be broken, that allies can turn into enemies in an instant.

What I see in these contributions is a set of ideas that has absorbed this reminder. Perhaps it changes your approach to know that someone here, where you live, has had to answer these questions before. What emerges, then, is not a declarative nationalism but something quieter: a steady belief in the sturdiness of an unfinished project.

I confess to you that I find no crisis in an unfinished project. On the contrary, I find possibility—something expansive, something you can always add to. It's tempting to look to the past for answers, but I am unconvinced that that's the best use of history. Instead, I have begun to look to the past for questions, because the best way we have to measure progress is to see if we are still asking the same questions after time has passed.

The bad news is that too many of the questions that move through *The New Romans* still move through *Elbows Up!* The good news is that our inheritance is never the answers, only the questions, and so conversely, the very best we can do is bequeath a new set of questions to the future. What follows represents our best attempt. May your questions be sharper still.

Elamin Abdelmahmoud
June 2025

MARGARET ATWOOD
The New Romans (1968)

Backdrop Addresses Cowboy

Star-spangled cowboy
sauntering out of the almost-
silly West, on your face
a porcelain grin, tugging a papier-mâché cactus
on wheels behind you with a string,

you are innocent as a bathtub
full of bullets.

Your righteous eyes, your laconic
trigger-fingers
people the streets with villains:
as you move, the air in front of you
blossoms with targets

and you leave behind you a heroic
trail of desolation:
beer bottles

slaughtered by the side
of the road, bird -
skulls bleaching in the sunset.

I ought to be watching
from behind a cliff or a cardboard storefront
when the shooting starts, hands clasped
in admiration,

but I am elsewhere.

Then what about me

what about the I confronting you on that border
you are always trying to cross?

I am the horizon
you ride towards, the thing you can never lasso

I am also what surrounds you:
my brain
scattered with your
tincans, bones, empty shells,
the litter of your invasions.

I am the space you desecrate
as you pass through.

On "Backdrop Addresses Cowboy"

I wrote "Backdrop Addresses Cowboy" in or around 1966, as Canadian self-awareness was cranking itself up. I should say "again"—Canadians' enthusiasm for themselves appears to be cyclical. In 1913, poet Pauline Johnson was revered, and her funeral was the largest Vancouver had ever seen. During the Great War, the Canadians were extolled—by themselves and others—when they captured Vimy Ridge; they never lost a battle after that. The Second World War was another high point, when Canadians fought up through Italy, and were then given the task of "clearing" the Netherlands. At the end of the war, Canada had the fourth-largest navy in the world.

But by the time I was in high school in the 1950s, things had changed. Having been joined at the hip with the British in the war, Canada saw those ties weakening, while connections with the United States—both commercial and cultural—grew stronger. Canadians' opinion of themselves shrank in comparison. New York was terrific, Toronto was a backwater, and so forth. We learned little about Canada in school—not the history, not the literature. In fact, it was a widespread belief that there wasn't any literature, apart from Stephen Leacock. Young writers were told as a matter of course that they should get out of the country and go to a place where writing was truly appreciated—London, Paris, New York. In 1963, when I was working for a market research company, the majority of Canadians in one of our surveys answered "No" to the question "Is there a difference between Canada and the United States?" Though they also answered "No" when asked if Canada should join the United States. It seems they knew there was a difference, but they didn't know what it was.

In the sixties, instead of leaving, many young writers decided to stay and, like beavers, rearrange their environment to make it more favourable to their pursuits. The early 1960s saw the creation of new magazines, then an uptick in the production of Canadian books and the promotion of Canadian authors, notably through the efforts of Jack McClelland of McClelland & Stewart. Later in the decade came the formation of new publishing companies: it seemed there was a readership for Canadian authors in Canada, after all. The success of Expo 67 increased the wave of pro-Canadian energy that had been building, accompanied as it was by a certain kind of anti-Americanism, which had its roots in young Americans' opposition to the Vietnam War. Al Purdy's anthology *The New Romans* was symptomatic. It included "Backdrop Addresses Cowboy."

Two more waves were to follow: the uproar around Brian Mulroney's Free Trade Agreement with the United States, with some for it (it would increase trade and benefit the economy) and some against it (it would make Canada too dependent on a very much larger and richer country to the south, in effect ceding control and creating unequal leverage; if they pulled the rug on such a deal after we'd become dependent on just one major trading partner—or rather, more dependent, as the flow of trade had already shifted to north–south from transatlantic—we would be up the proverbial creek without a paddle). I was of the latter party. People on opposite sides didn't come to blows, but they said harsh things, such as "I'll certainly never play bridge with THEM again." I've kept some artifacts from that time, including a T-shirt with a cartoon of an eagle having forced sexual congress with a beaver.

During the early and mid-sixties, I was studying in the United States, and getting an up-close-and-personal view not only of the seventeenth-century New England Puritans, but of the eighteenth-century land wars going on amongst the British and French, and then—come the American Revolution—between the soon-to-be Americans and the British. Manifest Destiny, westward expansion, and land-grab massacres of the original inhabitants were soon to follow, once those pesky treaties between Indigenous nations and the British Crown had been swept off the table.

One of the immediate inspirations for the poem was, however, a film I'd seen in the early sixties: *How the West Was Won* (1962). It had an all-star cast and was much celebrated at the time. The story is a familiar westward-expansion saga involving various hardships, family clashes, and cowboys-and-Indians shoot-'em-ups—standard myths of the times—underlaid with a belief that was once taken for granted: that wild lands and nature were there to be "won" or "conquered," and bent to the superior civilized will of the winners and conquerors. (Just like, you know, "women." Essentially passive and voiceless, without rights or any real being, clay to the potter's hand.) This was supposed to be in aid of "progress," which was one of the great shibboleths of the twentieth century. This is why I don't use the word *progressive*: change is not necessarily improvement, and eugenics—"progressive" in its time—was pretty awful, as were lobotomies. (Such a medical breakthrough. Probably developed through pithing frogs. But I digress.)

The end of the movie was jaw-dropping, at least for me. Against a background of lyric and celebratory music, and amongst panoramic views of other triumphs of engineering such as the Hoover Dam and the Golden Gate Bridge, was an aerial shot of a superhighway cloverleaf in Los Angeles, with cars going around and around it. This was the prize result of all that struggle and suffering and winning and conquering? Nature was to be killed, flattened, and erased for this? A superhighway cloverleaf? Eh? It seemed to me like a bathetic artistic choice. ("Bathos," says the *American Heritage Dictionary*, "is an abrupt, presumably unintended juxtaposition of the exalted and the commonplace, producing a ludicrous effect.")

So here we are again, in another iteration of Canadian self-esteem, but this time in the form of resistance to an existential threat. It seems that, according to the present American administration, Canada should be the new target of Manifest Destiny: inevitable and God-given American expansion is to flow northward, ignoring "artificial" borders and territories previously populated, erasing treaties, and I suppose—if deemed necessary—perpetrating massacres. At the very least we may expect a shootout on Bay Street, or a few summary hangings of die-hard federal MPs and the bombing of the Parliament Buildings in Ottawa. Then, after a while, someone will make a movie about it—*How the North Was Won*.

And, someone will write a poem inspired by it. Giving, perhaps, another perspective on the conquering and winning saga. A poem sort of like this one.

Nakedly Transactional

In the first few months after Donald Trump assumes the most powerful office on the planet for a second time, I notice a recurring theme in my correspondence. With increasing frequency, I receive message after message—from close friends, distant acquaintances, sometimes complete strangers—all urging me to leave the United States and come back to Canada. An organizer with a small literary festival off the B.C. coast tells me there's always room for my family on their small, picturesque island. My best friend in Toronto asks if she can reach out to academic institutions on my behalf to see if there's a job opening. A writer I've never met before sends a note about the quality of Vancouver's public schools. At first, the cynic in me is inclined to read these overtures as condescending, a strange by-product of the seething anger at Trump musing about turning Canada into the 51st state. But there is no condescension (though the anger is very real), only genuine concern. The novelist Paul Lynch once wrote that "history is a silent record of people who could not leave," and the notes I get come from people who truly believe this moment hovers now in the near horizon of American existence. For the first time since I arrived in this part of the world a quarter-century ago, the tenor of these U.S.-gazing conversations focuses not just on negation (*we are not like them*) or apology (*they're not really like this*) or bafflement (*I can't believe this is what they're like*), but something much more existential.

With almost every Canadian I talk to about the many deranged currents in which the United States is presently caught, there's a sense that the whole enterprise is collapsing. More and more, the phrase "before it's too late" becomes a fixture. And regardless of my own feelings about what collapse entails, or how regularly this enterprise has already collapsed onto the heads of its most vulnerable throughout its history, I find myself unable to disagree.

It just so happens I'm travelling across Canada for a book tour when Trump doubles down on his "51st state" comments (followed by a cartoonish series of tariff threats, backpedals, and more threats, the combination of which inspire more Canadian rage toward the U.S. government than I've ever witnessed in my lifetime). Overnight, every interview I do for my new book careens toward the subject of cross-border relations. It makes sense, and not only because it's a topic of conversation about which the country's media institutions are willing to indulge in a much greater level of anger than the book's other topics—in particular, the genocide of the Palestinian people, around which so many interviewers tiptoe with limitless caution. But not this; this is close. Canadians are furious, and rightly so. As so many descendants of this continent's earliest inhabitants can vouch, nobody likes seeing their home discussed as a site of acquisition, nobody likes seeing the treaties and agreements they've signed be ignored or unilaterally altered. Of course there's rage.

But there is something instructive about the undercurrent of astonishment that often accompanies this rage: *How could our closest ally behave in such a shamelessly transactional way?* In so much Canadian editorial coverage of this dispute, there are periodic reminders of just how inexplicable and self-inflicted this whole thing is—a decades-long bond between nations, so needlessly degraded.

And perhaps there should be astonishment, that the United States would go so far as to treat its closest neighbour, its closest friend—whatever the term of endearment may be—the same way it treats the vast majority of nations on this earth.

In November of 2024, I flew to the Qatari capital of Doha to teach a writing workshop. I grew up in this tiny peninsular state that periodically pops up in global headlines whenever its rulers manage to host a World Cup or gift the U.S. president a fancy plane. It was about a quarter-century since I had left as a teenager, bound for Canada. I wanted to go back and see the house I grew up in, the people I'd gone to school with, whose lives now in middle age had followed a far different trajectory than mine.

My month-long teaching gig was at Georgetown University's Doha campus. Years ago, the Qatari royal family offered a gaggle of North American schools a blank cheque to come build satellite facilities. Today, "Education City" on the outskirts of downtown is one of the most sprawling, well-funded academic operations I've ever seen. And as with the equally sprawling U.S. military base out in the Qatari desert, this country's ruling family doesn't just shell out obscene sums of money to keep these institutions humming out of the kindness of its heart. "Do you know what happens if they stop paying for that base?" one of my Education City colleagues asked me one day. "The Saudis invade tomorrow. Hell, the one thing that might keep them at bay is how much shit they'd get into if they damaged one of these American schools in the process."

It has always been this nakedly transactional. In countries like Qatar, in those tiny Pacific Island states that vote in lockstep with the U.S. on every United Nations resolution related to Palestine and Israel, in El Salvador and its rentable gulags, in the places where the bombing of a hospital provokes outrage and the places where it provokes no reaction at all. For all the idiocy of the present Trump administration, there's also a near-refreshing candour about its adherence to this way of doing things. Without the obligation of performative virtue, of any veneer of concern for human rights, there's no need to waste anyone's time. Canada becomes no more or less a friend or ally than Saudi Arabia. Friends and allies become useless concepts; there's only whoever happens to be sitting at the opposite end of the bargaining table, and what can be extracted from them. It makes for good speeches when presidents and prime ministers talk of special relationships between nations, but if all that talk is in the end an elaborate euphemism for states that happen to occupy mutually beneficial positions along the axis of capitalism and colonialism, much of this present moment makes perfect sense. There's a reason why, of all the arguments that have been levelled against Trump's policies, the one that seems to have found the most traction is simply that it's going to raise prices.

By the time my Canadian book tour comes to an end, the country feels changed. Canadian travel to the U.S. falls off a cliff; commercial and institutional boycotts, so often dismissed in other contexts as ineffective or illiberal, suddenly become tactics of mass patriotic appeal; at the highest political levels, there's talk of a new era, one in which this country works instead on strengthening its ties with other allies, ones that won't turn on a dime.

Maybe this sense that the United States is undergoing something terminal will last, and the relationship across the world's largest undefended border will never be the same. Or maybe it will prove far less effort to just ride this administration out, wait for someone more palatable to return to the White House, and keep things as they've been.

The young woman in the book-signing line was crying. Her friend had just been kidnapped, and she thought she might be next.

A couple of weeks after the end of the Canadian book tour, I travelled to Brookline, about a half-hour's drive west of Boston, for another event. Toward the end of the evening, a woman in her twenties came up to talk to me. She said she was a student at a nearby university, until recently active in the protest movement against the slaughter in Gaza. One of her friends, who'd written an op-ed calling for divestment from Israel, had just been snatched off the street by federal agents. At the time, hardly anyone knew where she had been taken, the conditions of her capture, the details of her supposed crime.

There had been other such kidnappings—indeed, they quickly became a hallmark of the early days of the second Trump presidency. In the weeks and months to come, there'd be more. The purpose was not so much to punish those who were taken as to prompt terror in those who were not. "I think they might come for me too," the young woman in Brookline kept saying, "I think they might come for me too."

I had no idea what to tell her. There's little use prognosticating; who knows what comes next? By the time this book is published, everything in this essay might feel a million years old, buried under whatever calamities are to come. Is it the case that something in the North American dynamic has been irreparably broken, and there really is an entirely new set of political and economic relationships to be forged? Or is this only a temporary chill, to be followed inevitably by more speeches about common faith in common ideals.

In truth, I think about leaving the United States all the time, about Lynch's description of history, and all those people who waited too long, who ultimately could not leave. And then I think about far less apocalyptic, far more prosaic concerns: finances, social circles, employment prospects, all those stubborn sites of inertia that keep people tethered to the same relationships, year after year, decade after decade. Perhaps the same is true of nations as well.

Canada Needs a Rewrite

For years, the Hudson's Bay Company charter stood outside the corporate boardroom at the company's downtown Toronto headquarters at 401 Bay Street. I was often one of several dozen people who passed its glass case as we filed in and out of meetings about company strategy. I don't remember anyone sparing it a glance. In fact, the dun-coloured document struck me as one of the least impressive of the company's artifacts: no competition for the taxidermized animals or the *coureur de bois* mannequins in their HBC blanket coats that led the way to the company cafeteria in Brampton. As a child, if you asked me to name the country's most important artifact I would probably have chosen one of the mummies at the Royal Ontario Museum. The Royal Charter that gave HBC explorers the right to invade Canada had no such gravitas, even though it was signed on deerskin.

Americans keep their Declaration of Independence proudly displayed in the National Archives in Washington, D.C.; the Canadian equivalent is sitting in a storage room somewhere.

Maybe that's fitting. The Declaration of Independence is a list of demands and an articulation of values declaring the beginning of a country. HBC's Royal Charter, like so many letters and ledgers and other records in the official company archives, is a trade agreement: a document forged between the Crown and explorers before Confederation. Now, it's potentially up for sale, one of the last tangible items in the sell-off of HBC.

I had an average—to say, pitiful—understanding of Canadian history when I went to work at Hudson's Bay in 2009. According to what I had learned in high school, Canada was founded by two great cultures—the French and the English—who followed the river routes with the best of intentions. I joined the company as head copywriter, aka "Chief Adventurer of Writing," just as the Bay and other heritage department stores were going through an international boom. My job was to oversee everything from product names to the messages that appeared on billboards—and dozens, if not hundreds, of seasonal and annual ad campaigns. We also worked on books and longer-term projects, such as campaigns for the Olympics and the Hudson's Bay point blanket. Over the next six years, I discerned a much truer picture of the company's history with the Crown, its relationship to trade, and the country's treatment of Indigenous people.

As the story goes, once Canada was founded through a real estate deal that saw the transfer of land from the Hudson's Bay Company to the Crown and then to the new country of Canada, HBC sold land packages to settlers like my Scottish great-great-grandparents. The company developed further through such transactions, providing mail-order goods to fill the houses that were going up, and eventually became a department store chain serving big cities. By the time American real estate magnate Richard Baker took over HBC in 2008, he was acquiring a brand with a logo almost as recognized as Canada's itself; internally, the Bay prided itself on being "the company that became a nation." Over the next decade, Baker sold off the land under the Bay locations, and thus reduced the value of its holdings, piece by piece. Now, the most truly valuable thing left—a document worth everything and nothing—is the charter. HBC is being absorbed back into the land it came from, just like my father, whose body we lowered into a family plot last winter in Harris, Saskatchewan, out near our old family farm.

Canada is built on real estate. That's how Don Gillmor, author of *Canada: A People's History*, described the Bay when he wrote a story for *The Walrus* about the 2022 donation of the long-time Winnipeg flagship store to the Southern Chiefs' Organization: "Canada's oldest company began as a land deal (at least from the European perspective) during an outbreak of the bubonic plague and may end as a real estate deal in another plague."

That's how U.S. president Donald Trump sees this country too: as a "beautiful land mass," as he posted to his followers on Truth Social this past April 28, Canada's election day. "No more artificially drawn line from many years ago," he said, referring to the 49th parallel, also the world's longest undefended border, as evidence of his case for annexing Canada to the U.S.

In spite of his incredible chutzpah, Trump clearly sees Canada for what it always has been—a colossal real estate grab. Someone has owned Canada for the last 355 years. Why shouldn't it be his?

I must sound angry. Should I be? This is the way people have always done it here. Canada is just the first developer's dream.

The problem is that we keep putting real estate over people.

Canada celebrated its 150th birthday in 2017 through a series of national events. *The Walrus*, where I was soon to become editor-in-chief, held public talks across the country on the theme of "We Desire a Better Country." Every set of speakers included a recipient of the Order of Canada as well as an Indigenous leader. I tried to attend as many of the talks as I could. What struck me was that, in every instance I attended in person, an Indigenous speaker said some version of "Canada is not my country." In Charlottetown, P.E.I., the site of Confederation, Teyotsihstokwáthe Dakota Brant said, "The irony is not [lost] on me that I am here because I've been identified as an exceptional Canadian. I have never, nor have my ancestors ever, asked for that moniker."

It can't have been the first time I heard that view expressed—many Indigenous writers and activists share similar views—but it was the first time I had heard it said on a public stage, under the Canadian flag, in a room full of Canadian celebrities and, if I remember correctly, the province's lieutenant governor and their kilt-wearing detail. It was also the encapsulation of an insight I'd been reaching for in a lifetime of trying to encapsulate Canada for Canadians: it was as if someone had pointed out the emperor's new clothes, something most of us are afraid to say.

Canada is not a thing. It's a concept you can buy into—or, in the case of Dakota Brant (who was crowned Miss Indian World in 2010), choose not to. What if we all just came out and said it? Canada is not a thing. Or at least, it's not one fixed, permanent concept. To admit it openly would make what we are more authentic, instead of an ideal to chase. We could make Canada's opt-in identity intentional, like when Gwyneth Paltrow rebranded divorce as "conscious uncoupling."

All my life, it's felt as if we're all trying to build up Canada into something bigger than it is. As a young journalist it was my job to cover restaurants and designers and profile Canadian "ones to watch" as if the subjects were Hollywood stars; I realized the product we were selling was a vision of Canada itself. The more I become a professional "expert" on Canada, the less convinced I am that we are alike or that we need to be. I've thought this through jobs at the *Globe and Mail* ("Canada's National Newspaper"), Hudson's Bay ("Canada's Department Store"), *The Walrus* ("Canada's Conversation"), and more recently, while conducting a national research project on the CBC/Radio-Canada, our national public media service.

If Canada were a thing, chances are you and I wouldn't be able to agree on how to define it anyway. Do you like hockey? Do you love seeing plays at the Stratford Festival? Chances are the same person does not love both of those things, but in Canada, we're all supposed to be fiddling and drinking beer and wearing red plaid shirts the same long endless day. I'm tired of it. I would happily stake my personal Canada on homemade bread from Saskatchewan, watching the crashing waves on the beach in Ucluelet, and Ontario apples and cranberries. Your list would include different things. It doesn't mean we can't both be Canadian. But let's not write a story—let alone build a national identity—out of a series of Instagram posts.

There's a beer-and-hockey-commercial version of the country that has had a resurgence since the tariff talk came up. And it's easy to buy into. "Elbows up." In the face of threat, Canadians are rushing to a show of strength. But while the instinct is admirable, I would be wary of using simplistic definitions of what "Canadian" is to define where we go next. First of all, the best-known images we have were invented to sell us products like beer (see, for example, the resurgence of the "I Am Canadian" ad, which has its distant origins in an Australian Qantas campaign). And I, too, cry at Tim Hortons commercials depicting weary parents driving too-young offspring to hockey practice in the grey morning hours. But I think the reason they move us is that they demonstrate perseverance under hardship, just as we're facing today.

The problem with such lifestyle-oriented images of Canada is that they leave so many people out. A lot of newcomers to Canada don't play hockey. If you didn't grow up playing—or can't afford it—it's hard to pick it up. While editing *The Walrus*, I was also struck by an audience survey that found the same proportion of people thought that poetry and hockey were "very important." Whatever your passion is, it may look like a niche interest to someone else.

I didn't really understand Canada in its complexity until 2023, when I was approached by McGill University's Centre for Media, Technology, and Democracy to lead "What Should the CBC/Radio-Canada Be?" Soon after, Conservative leader Pierre Poilievre threatened to defund or cancel Canada's public media service if elected prime minister. My colleagues and I decided to ask Canadians themselves what they wanted from the CBC. It turned out that 78 per cent of Canadians wanted to keep it, especially if it could address the major criticisms levelled against it.

It is harder to find consensus about what to do with the outlet. About the same number of people think the CBC/Radio-Canada is "too woke" (27 per cent) and not "too woke" (31 per cent). About one quarter (23 per cent) of Canadians agreed with the statement that the CBC/Radio-Canada is "irrelevant", with 39 per cent holding the reverse opinion that it is not "irrelevant." When we asked if the CBC/Radio-Canada were better suited to be a news organization, a cultural hub, or both, a minority of people chose one of the first scenarios while a majority (53 per cent) said both. That's the Canada that feels familiar—a place full of people who like different things. Speak different languages. Have different needs. One of the biggest aspects that divides us is not age, gender, or political identity—it's where we live. The only thing I'm sure we agree on, based on my experience at the Bay, is a desire for well-fitting, affordable jeans.

And that's the problem with simplistic definitions of this country and many proposals for what to do with the broadcaster—such as whether to make it opt-in for those who can afford to pay, or to do away with television programming, or to do away with digital content. If you don't like the CBC, it kind of means you don't like Canada—Canada as it is, not as it's portrayed in commercials and memes (urban, affluent, educated, English-speaking). No, Canada is not a convenient country to live in; in comparison with others, it's large, relatively underpopulated, expensive, and multi-faceted.

All that complexity doesn't mean that a quality of Canadian life isn't worth fighting for. Countries that fight hard end up being too difficult to take.

My Canada is a real estate agreement between people who have contracted to live together under common goals: health-care, say, or religious tolerance. These are good things. I don't know that there's much to take from other countries around the world that are better than that—not without losing something about other people's right to be. When I see what looks like a "healthy" nationalism in some parts of the world, I see how it disavows alternate narratives.

And so we come back to the problem of America, which has radically changed its tune.

In early 2025, U.S. president Donald Trump unexpectedly announced his desire to make Canada the "cherished 51st state." The immediate response for many of us here wasn't emotional or patriotic outrage; it was to think of the physical threat. I was surprised to find out in the following days how many of my friends and family members had discussions about where they could evacuate to if that happened, and what they'd bring. That's where our minds go when someone threatens to invade Canada, because it's been going there all along.

My partner, who was a soldier once, quipped that Canada is too big and wild to conquer, regions like Toronto too dense and populated to be easily occupied. He said this to me and his son, my stepson, as if this should be comforting. It was terrify-ing! I think what he meant was: Canada is designed to resist this kind of U.S. invasion.

One baking hot summer day, we stopped in Kingston to visit Fort Henry, the naval base built on Lake Ontario after the War of 1812. At that time, a U.S. invasion of Canada had looked feasible, even likely; the British installed the fort to protect the

Rideau Canal and the way to the Canadian capital, along with other trade routes. Fortuitously, the fort was never used for that purpose; it is now a national historic site. On that trip, I stood at the top of the eerily deserted pile of bricks, white and shimmering in the mid-day heat, next to a cannon pointed out over the water. With the American side so close, you can see how real it is. Perhaps because it's so real, after 1812, the Americans didn't bother trying.

America's relationship with Canada is a story, also. It has plot twists. A few short years ago, Canadian prime minister Justin Trudeau and U.S. president Barack Obama were taking selfies together. Now a lot of us have changed our vacations and grocery orders. What is Canada without the United States? One of the biggest fictions about the concept of Canada is the notion that America was going to protect us forever. We just thought they would.

The story of Canada is the story that people choose to tell.

Some people get uneasy when I bring up the subject of "what is Canada?" I think talking about it threatens us. That's why we don't do away with the monarchy, even though about equal numbers of Canadians now either want or don't want to do that. When we say anarchic things about the country, and someone reacts, I don't think it's because they disagree with the criticisms other people have—they just don't have a story to replace it. There is literally a giant abyss of unsolved questions about what we'd be without our Canadian narrative.

As a writer and editor, I am used to the idea that for every story, there are ten possible ways to tell it. Maybe I take what is presented to me as a draft: we can start at the ending and then work backwards. Or we can start at the beginning and work chronologically. If Canada is a story, that means all of us can rewrite it.

Can we afford to give up our story and write a new one? Can we afford not to? I was in Toronto when the Blue Jays first won the World Series in 1992. Cars honked and drove up and down. I think it was the happiest day of my brother's life. We all felt that something had shifted. We were the winners, not the losers. It was a victory for the Blue Jays, but a step for Canada as well. For so long, we'd been the country that got an honourable mention. Now, Canada was in first place.

The emotions we feel at such times, the kinship with each other, are real. Just like the ties that have strengthened between us in the face of America's threat are real. The love I felt in the pandemic, when a neighbour came out on his balcony and for some reason chose to play "O Canada" on his trumpet, leaving a lump in my throat, was real; and because all the people on the street screamed and clapped so much, he did it twice in a row for the following eighty-five nights till he discontinued it from exhaustion. That was real. That is Canada.

To save the best of that true love—what is real—we might have to move on. Fight for Canada not as it was, not the real estate–focused place it is, but the country it should become.

After all, how can the best of Canada survive if we don't find an ending that works?

Like Moths to a Flame

As long as Canadian stories are worth making into films, Americans will be sent into Canada to make them.

Lewis Selznick, Hollywood producer
of the early twentieth century

On St. Patrick's Day, 1985, U.S. president Ronald Reagan appeared on stage with Canadian prime minister Brian Mulroney to signal the beginning of a new era of Canada–U.S. relations. It was Reagan's first foreign appearance since his re-election, and the visit was intended to heal a rupture between Washington and Ottawa left behind by the departing government of Prime Minister Pierre Trudeau.

Diplomatic records of the time describe the relationship between Reagan and Trudeau as "awkward," which is an understatement. Trudeau was openly disdainful of Reagan, whom he accused of prolonging the Cold War. Trudeau's contempt for the president was reflected in the anti-American mood of the Canadians at the time, who had booed Reagan on his last visit to Ottawa and set American flags on fire.

Newly elected prime minister Brian Mulroney was a very different political animal and determined to make Ron feel at home. In Quebec City, Reagan and Mulroney engaged like old friends, though they had met only once before. Along with their wives, Mila and Nancy, who were bedecked in shimmering green evening gowns, they joined opera singer Maureen Forrester in a schmaltzy rendition of "When Irish Eyes Are Smiling," billed as a tribute to the shared ethnic heritage of the two men as they cemented their friendship.

Canadian historian Jack Granatstein said that the "public display of sucking up to Reagan may have been the single most demeaning moment in the entire political history of Canada's relations with the United States." But the Shamrock Summit, as it came to be called, was much more than cringe-inducing kitsch. It was the closing act of a carefully choreographed entente launching one of the most consequential developments in North American history: the Canada–U.S. free trade negotiations. When the pact was completed three years later, it fundamentally changed Canada's relationship with the economic giant to the south, yoking our two countries together in an ill-balanced alliance—the effects of which we are acutely feeling today. The existential threat to our sovereignty we face in 2025 began on that stage in Quebec City forty years ago.

"The eyes of all America are on Canada," Reagan had said in a speech delivered a day earlier. "There's a saying I've always liked," he continued, with his Hollywood drawl. "One should keep old roads and old friends. You have not strayed from the roads of Canadian culture, from those good and graceful virtues that enrich your lives and keep you free to be kind and true . . . We're with you, Mr. Prime Minister. We feel mighty grateful for Canada, and we always will."

For those attempting to make a living in "Canadian culture," the references in Reagan's speech were both risible and worrisome. American cultural imperialism was already a decades-old reality, with American players dominating all of English-language North America. And the U.S. entertainment industry routinely kiboshed the efforts of Canadian filmmakers, scriptwriters, book and periodical publishers, and music producers who wanted access not to U.S. markets, but to their own in Canada.

Worrisome as well because it quickly became clear that American media corporations would pounce on the opportunity of the trade talks to ensure that, going forward, nothing would impede their profits. They wanted to dismantle laws that gave preference to Canadian producers; to defang regulators that monitored Canadian content; and to shrink the effects of granting agencies that allowed artists, writers, and filmmakers the bare means to survive in a country whose population was so small. Brian Mulroney had barely sung the last note of "Irish Eyes" before media moguls in New York and Los Angeles were rubbing their hands in glee.

In 2025, Donald Trump has propelled Canadians into a ferocious outburst of nationalism just as Ronald Reagan and the free trade negotiations sent the nation spinning in 1985. Back then, after years of watching our sovereignty being chipped away, we were faced with the prospect that Canada was about to be formally absorbed into an American-dominated common culture. And the fear of losing our independence ignited the same existential questions as we pose today: Who are we as Canadians? What is our relationship with the elephant south of the border? And do we have the courage or even the desire to resist assimilation?

In 1985, as the free trade talks began, Margaret Atwood had just published *The Handmaid's Tale*; the CBC's *Anne of Green Gables* series had become the most watched Canadian TV drama in history; Sandy Wilson's movie *My American Cousin* was doing well at the box office; *SCTV* had wrapped up its last season, with Eugene Levy, Martin Short, and John Candy moving on to even greater roles; and k.d. lang was stealing hearts as the most promising female vocalist at the Juno Awards. We were just getting started, and it all seemed in peril.

That year was an inflection point for Canada, but it was also one for me personally. I had an eight-year-old boy, and I wondered if he would grow up as a Canadian or as an American. I was a freelance journalist, covering arts and culture at the time, and I set out on a quest to see what we were up against; to determine if we had the right stuff to resist what many believed would be the end of Canada as we knew it.

I have to suppress an instinctive boredom when I hear the words Canadian culture. I don't feel that when I hear the words British culture, or French or American. Only the words Canadian culture can produce in me that churn of nauseous ennui. How did this happen? Where does it come from? And who is it benefitting?

Excerpt from a 1985 speech in Kitchener, Ontario, by Canadian playwright John Gray

———

In the early winter of 1985, I had an interview with Thomas Niles, the U.S. ambassador to Canada. The American embassy in Ottawa would later move to a fortress-like structure near the ByWard Market, but at that time it was still housed in a charming art nouveau building on Wellington Street. Ambassador Niles was sprawled in his elegant office; large (certainly bulletproof) windows looked out toward the Peace Tower on Parliament Hill. I was speaking with him not long after the trade talks had been announced, and I got my first taste of the arguments that we would hear for the next three years.

"My impression is that the people of Canada want to hear Canadian voices but they don't want to be cut off from the culture of other countries," the ambassador told me. He had arrived at his Canadian post only months earlier, appointed as the overlord of the trade talks. And apparently he came with a full knowledge of our hearts and minds.

"The Soviet Union has decided, since the 1920s, to have rigid control over the cultural life of the country," he continued. The Cold War was a daily reality at that time, and its every mention was meant to strike fear into the hearts of freedom-loving people. But to compare our puny efforts to protect Canadian culture to that of Stalin seemed a bit over the top. "There's a price you pay," he warned. "You have to weigh these things."

Ambassador Niles was leading America's lobbyists, who had two objectives—unfettered access to Canadian fossil fuel products and unfettered access to Canadian cultural industries. There really wasn't much else the U.S. wanted from us that they didn't already have. Greater access to oil and gas production was easily obtained, but the American negotiators suspected they might have to pry ownership of our culture from our tight little fingers.

American media producers had long regarded our precious attachment to our culture as a commercial irritant, and legal counsel for all the major arts and entertainment multinationals saw the trade talks as a long-awaited opportunity to dismantle what Canada had put in place to support its artists. The Americans demanded unimpeded access to our markets for everything from children's books to blockbuster movies. As a bonus, their victory with Canada would also send a message to other countries not to ever get in their way.

Canada had much more at stake in the negotiations than the U.S. did, and it became increasingly obvious that Mulroney was ready to bet the store on winning a deal that he claimed would make us all rich beyond our wildest dreams. He repeatedly insisted that he would not sell our soul to the devil, but right from the beginning there was a problem with language. What we called "culture" American negotiators claimed was "business." What we called "cultural identity" was what they considered a "non-tariff trade barrier." What we called our "sovereignty," Americans called "hogwash." And it wasn't certain that Mulroney thought differently, or that he would stand up to some of the most powerful people in the United States— people who were tight with his new BFF, Ronald Reagan.

In polls taken at the time, most Canadians claimed they wanted their culture protected. But what did that mean? And what were they willing to pay? Artists could paint, write, film, dance, and perform their little hearts out, but they could never be effective, or make a living, if no one knew who they were and if they didn't have access to an audience. Certainly in

Quebec, culture was regarded as a vital part of identity, embedded with the French language, and it was fiercely guarded. But English Canadians would be tested by these trade talks. And Mulroney suspected that, if it came down to having cheaper stuff, winter homes in Florida, and tariff-free markets for cedar shakes and shingles, they might be willing to sacrifice *The Littlest Hobo* or to give up on the idea of ever seeing Canadian movies at their cinemas. They had likely never watched one anyway.

Richard Olsen, senior counsel for CBS TV, met with me just as he and other high-powered lawyers began lobbying the Canada–U.S. trade negotiators. With corporate New York condescension, Olsen sneered when I challenged him about the value of the arts in Canada. "What are these distinctive Canadian cultural values that I hear so much about in general terms?" he asked me. "I'm never told how these Canadian values differ from the rest of the western world."

For Olsen, Canadian national identity and cultural sovereignty were simply buzzwords—a smokescreen. Our content quotas for music and television stood in the way of U.S. producers. Canadians loved U.S. shows and music, he said. We imitated them, and then we had the audacity to pass laws limiting our American cousins from making an honest buck in our country. We were pirates, Olsen told me. "The worst offenders in the world."

I later attended a three-day event at the University of Windsor at which American and Canadian stakeholders in the free trade talks came to debate "Cultural Sovereignty: Myth or Reality." I could see the Ambassador Bridge from the meeting room—an impressive suspension arc over the Detroit River where a steady stream of transport trucks moved millions of dollars in goods every day. Thomas Niles had sent his deputy, James Thurber, whose stated mission was to reassure Canadians that there was no such thing as American cultural imperialism.

"That an outside force can influence a nation's culture is almost ludicrous," Thurber told the audience. Canadians needed to get out of their garrison mentality, he said. The War of 1812 was over. It was time to meet our natural destiny with the continent. Thurber also introduced a new talking point, consistent with the "cultural communism" trope. He announced somewhat ominously that any effort to restrict American media into Canada would be regarded by the U.S. as censorship, "and you don't want that."

During conversations with Americans that year, I often found their arguments to be weak and ill-conceived, failing to read the Canadian room. This was the case when Thurber added a bizarre analogy to his presentation—one that he obviously thought would hit the mark but just left us scratching our heads: "It's like saying keep all the Emily Carr works in Canada. Don't let them come to the United States. They might influence us in the wrong way. I don't think Canadians believe that the flowering of their culture depends on being isolated from American culture."

I was brought up in Truro, Nova Scotia. For us, the world was a distant flame from the south; hot, bright, dancing and utterly fascinating. We experienced this mythic flame as a vaguely tantalizing light that glowed somewhere over the horizon, giving

off a distant, unsatisfying warmth. The flame glowed brightly when
we went to the movies or watched TV or listened to the hit parade.
But as soon as the movie was over we were back in Truro. Which
seemed more cold and drab than it had before.

John Gray

For a time in the early twentieth century, before Hollywood's major studios developed a global monopoly on movie production, Canada actually had a viable domestic film business. The world war years were a time of patriotism that brought on a curiosity about our own people and their stories. Canadian movie producers raised money, made movies, and then showed them in Canadian cinemas. There were a lot of dog sleds, damsels-in-distress being rescued from ice floes, and the cinema's first nude scene, but in a goofy way those movies were distinctly Canadian. It didn't last long.

The major Hollywood studios will insist that they came to dominate our movie industry simply because Americans offered a superior product. But the real economic advantage was something called vertical integration. The U.S. companies in Los Angeles that made the movies bought up film distribution networks all over North America. And—the grand prize—they established an almost complete monopoly over exhibition. The same companies that made the films owned the movie houses, where they allowed no films but their own to have screentime. Canada was simply regarded as an extension of the American market. Independent films, Canadian and otherwise, are even today almost non-existent on their playbills.

Throughout the twentieth century, Canadian film producers pleaded with Ottawa to issue laws that would break up what was clearly a cartel. Other countries had done so, but Canada was reluctant. Politicians suspected that the movie moguls in Hollywood might refuse to show their products in Canada if there was any opposition—they often threatened to do so. The thought of being the minister responsible for denying Canadians the next Hollywood blockbuster was too much to contemplate.

In the 1940s, C.D. Howe, known as the "Minister of Everything," offered a ludicrous compromise. If Hollywood occasionally mentioned something about Canada in their movies, this might satisfy the Canadian desire to see ourselves reflected on the silver screen. In films from the 1940s and '50s, you might notice references that seem to come from nowhere—mentions of the "Canadian Rockies" or "red-winged black birds, from Canada." Those meaningless lines were the glass beads we took in exchange for our entire movie distribution rights. From time to time, Hollywood actually made movies with Canadian stories; Hollywood legend Lewis Selznick had said it might happen if there was a Canadian story worth telling. Roy Rogers and his horse Trigger turned up in British Columbia in *North of the Great Divide*, which was among several movies starring the Mounties. But that's about it.

Canada established federal agencies that were supposed to help make domestic films, but they had little effect. The National Film Board did a good job, but it had no place to show its material. Telefilm Canada's assignment was to administer private and public money for film and television production. Again, there was almost no place to put the final product. The government gave substantial tax breaks to private investors, which mostly resulted in lawyers and dentists getting rich on making movies like *Porky's*, a silly soft-porn comedy that is set in nowhere. *Porky's* was one of the rare Canadian movies to get distribution, but that was entirely because Hollywood considered it one of their own. It became the highest-grossing Canadian film in history.

In the 1970s, the Canadian government tried to force Canadian television networks, including the CBC, to show more Canadian-made programs. The networks balked. News and current affairs programs were robust and popular, but Canadian-made drama and sitcoms consisted of modestly popular fare like *The Beachcombers* and *King of Kensington*—mostly made by the CBC, and so profit from advertising wasn't the only driving force. Almost all programs on the Canadian primetime schedule were American, including those on the CBC.

Private television networks insisted they could actually make a profit from Canadian programs, but only if the government shielded them from any American competition. And so Ottawa protected their market, giving them an exclusive monopoly over the Canadian airwaves. But our broadcasters rarely lived up to their end of the bargain. When CRTC licenses came up for renewal, the executives would shuffle their feet, admit they had failed, and promise to do better next year. They never did. After an approval, they would carry on making mountains of profits until the next renewal period. Canadian private broadcasting was little more than a licence to print money.

One afternoon, I went to see Global TV's president Paul Morton to ask him, in not so many words, how he was able to sleep at night. The return on investment in Canadian broadcasting was 30 per cent. No other industry in the country came even close to that. Broadcasters like Global made inexpensive programs with government subsidies that were designed mostly to get licences renewed. They showed those programs late at night after everyone was in bed, a CanCon ghetto that came to be called the "beaver hours."

"We cannot be elitist," Morton told me. "We cannot say, this is what you must see. We must provide what they want to see, which is American programs."

Canadian companies were buying up big-budget American television series—paying, for example, $100,000 for an episode of *Dallas* that had cost the U.S. producers a million dollars to make. Then the Canadian broadcasters slapped their own ads on those shows and watched the money roll in, relying on the big U.S. publicity machines to draw in bigger audiences.

Morton knew it was indefensible. But he ultimately blamed Canadians. "I'm only being half facetious when I say that I think it should be outlawed to advertise or have reported that any program is Canadian in origin. We'd have a better job attracting audiences. Canadians have an inferiority complex." He could offer me no credible reason why the Americans should not gobble up our TV broadcasting companies.

Over at CTV, it wasn't much better. Executive Doug Bassett defended CTV's record, noting that they were paying $135,000 an episode to make *The Littlest Hobo*, the only Canadian-made program he could point to with anything like enthusiasm.

"What are you most proud of, then?" I asked him.

"I can't tell you what I'm proud of," he replied, squirming.

"Why not?"

"I don't know the programs! I don't watch CTV twenty-four hours a day! How should I know?" He finally admitted that *The Cosby Show* was his favourite. "Everybody loves *The Cosby Show*!"

I reminded him that Bill Cosby and his sitcom were American.

"I know. But how can we do that in Canada?" Bassett snapped. "There's no talent here. There are no writers."

"Where are the writers?

"They've all gone to the United States."

"Can you get them back?"

A deep sigh. "No."

By the 1980s, so many talented Canadians had left for the states that Los Angeles was estimated to be, in population numbers, the fifth-largest Canadian city.

To make the point, dozens of Canadians working in the States got together in 1985 to make a mockumentary called *The Canadian Conspiracy*, a movie that spoofs both U.S. anti-Soviet propaganda and American investigative journalism. Eugene Levy plays a jittery whistleblower, sheltered in a darkened hotel room where he spills the beans on the alleged espionage.

The storyline is that the Canadian government has infiltrated the U.S., conquering its soul, sending wave upon wave of Canadian actors, writers, and producers to Hollywood and New York as fifth columnists. Americans have been sucked into a nefarious plot, and Eugene Levy tells all. Every American hero, from Pa Cartwright to Perry Mason to Captain Kirk, is exposed by Levy as not only a Canadian, but one who has insinuated their way into the American entertainment industry under Ottawa's direction.

The film is hilarious—it showed on the CBC at the height of the free trade talks—and features John Candy, Martin Short, Leslie Nielsen, Lorne Michaels, Margot Kidder, Tommy Chong, Lorne Greene, Dan Ackroyd, and Donald Sutherland among a dozen other "secret agents," many of whom had worked with Canadian Lorne Michaels on *Saturday Night Live*, a program that Levy exposes as part of the subversion.

Americans did not get the joke. But *The Canadian Conspiracy* was wildly popular in Canada, like a secret handshake. The added irony is that in 2025 comedian Mike Myers gave Canadians the call to arms "Elbows up!" on SNL, a program built almost entirely with Canadian talent. (And it goes without saying that Myers's movie *Wayne's World* should have been set in a basement rec room in Scarborough, Ontario, not in a suburb of Illinois.)

Why should we tell our audiences that there is a distinct society here with a history and culture that is worth looking at? Who are we to tell audiences that we are interesting people? That this is an interesting place to live? And yet we can, you know? Canada has something to say. We could light our own flame.

John Gray

There's a delightful photo in the CBC's archives: a picture of Stompin' Tom Connors, Anne Murray, the Mercy Brothers, and Myrna Lorrie all holding their prizes from the very first Juno Awards in 1971. Standing among them, in a business suit, is one of the dullest men that I have ever interviewed. He was also one of the most influential and among my favourite people.

In 1970, Pierre Juneau, for whom the award is named, imposed Canadian content regulations on broadcasters in Canada that actually had teeth, compelling them to play 30 per cent Canadian music on their airwaves or lose their licences. Radio broadcasters were apoplectic. This was not what their listeners wanted. But Juneau was not for turning. There are conflicting views on the value of CanCon regulations, but there is no denying that many of the artists we know and love today not only got airtime as a result but were able to make their recordings in Canadian studios. The Canadian industry boomed.

I can recall sitting in an office with Pierre Juneau, but I have no surviving transcripts or tape from that encounter. Aside from remembering that he was gracious and generous with his time, there was absolutely nothing notable about talking with a man who helped to put Anne Murray, Lighthouse, Blood, Sweat & Tears, Bruce Cockburn, The Guess Who, Edward Bear, Gordon Lightfoot, Leonard Cohen, Ian & Sylvia, and Crowbar on the charts.

Pierre Trudeau had appointed Juneau to the CRTC with a mandate to Canadianize the airwaves, and he did so. (He had less success with the TV networks.) In the 1980s, Mulroney replaced Juneau with André Bureau, a man who had little time for CanCon regulations and who once told me that Canadians should be able to choose their entertainment; not have it imposed on them. Suffice it to say, there are no awards called the Buros.

Juneau was dull but he had balls. He went on to be one of the best CBC presidents the broadcaster ever had. Trudeau appointed him to the CBC in 1982, and over the next five years Juneau increased Canadian content on its airwaves to 95 per cent, refused to put ads back on CBC Radio, and introduced Newsworld as the Canadian alternative to U.S. all-news channels. Millions of people watched and listened to Canadian content on the CBC thanks to Juneau. Market forces be damned.

In the 1980s, we also had a thriving magazine industry— *Maclean's*, *Saturday Night*, and *Chatelaine* among them—that was subsidized and protected one way or another by the government. The world knows the writings of Mordecai Richler, Margaret Atwood, Leonard Cohen, Pierre Berton, Margaret Laurence, and Farley Mowat because publisher Jack McClelland invented CanLit and made Canadian literature famous. The work was stellar of course. But the publisher McClelland & Stewart relied on government subsidies and protected Canadian ownership for its survival.

At the same time, the performing arts thrived; our theatre and dance troupes were celebrated around the world. Critics from the United States and Europe made the pilgrimage to Canada, where they reviewed our visual arts; painters and sculptors peddled their work abroad. For some, it became profitable but, while many will attempt to deny it, hardly an artist, writer, or producer in this country could have succeeded in Canada without the benefit of some taxpayer support.

The free trade talks posed an enormous threat to Canadian culture, but it was always—one way or another—subject to the whims of the government of the day. Cultural survival in Canada is a perpetual game of snakes and ladders. And, in 1985, it was one long snake.

———

Whenever the Mulroney government was challenged about culture during the negotiations, its ministers would insist that our cultural "identity" was not on the free trade table. But when asked if cultural "industries" were up for grabs, the ministers would dodge and weave. Before the talks even began, the government offered to rewrite legislation that was critical to the support of the Canadian periodical and newspaper industries. By law, Canadian publications had advantages in the advertising market that were denied to U.S. competitors, a hard-won concession that had allowed Canadian material to compete on a level playing field. Mulroney was ready to give it away to American negotiators as a goodwill gesture, like sacrificing a lamb. News of the offer was leaked; and the law survived.

One of the rare occasions of a politician having the courage to go up against the Hollywood movie majors was actually Flora MacDonald, a minister in Mulroney's own government. In 1986, she introduced a bill that would force Hollywood-owned movie houses in Canada to give over just a fraction of their screentime to Canadian movies. It was a cheeky move, given that free trade talks were ongoing. But MacDonald had the audacity to test Mulroney's assertion that culture was not on the table. She soon found out the truth. Jack Valenti, the Dark Prince of Hollywood lobbyists and probably the most powerful man in the entertainment business, simply made a phone call to his friend Ronald Reagan, and that was the end of it. MacDonald's bill was withdrawn; to this day, there has never been another attempt of its kind.

When the multinational Gulf and Western bought the global textbook publisher Prentice-Hall in 1986, Canada initially demanded that the U.S. company divest the Canadian branch, in accordance with Canadian law. Gulf and Western literally threatened "a scorched earth response" if it couldn't get its way. The Mulroney government quickly backed down. As Ottawa insisted our culture was not for sale, 80 per cent of the profits from book publishing were going south.

Bit by bit, we were losing ground, with the Mulroney government banking on the assumption that Canadians would do anything to get access to those U.S. markets—and that it didn't really matter where our books, movies, or television came from.

The word *conquest* came up a lot during that era of protests against the trade talks. But in the course of my year of talking to people, I never got an impression that most Canadians really cared much about their culture or the intangible thing called a "Canadian identity." A stalwart core of Canadian nationalists, mostly made up of trade unionists, environmentalists, and artists who understood what was at stake, showed up for demonstrations and made a lot of noise. But it seemed to me that the will to nationhood in Canada was generally not strong, and that we were our own worst enemy. Quebec was different; Quebecers valued their culture as the safeguard of their language. But English Canadians had a complex when it came to our culture. I came to think that Canada didn't need an identity, it needed a shrink.

I first met John Hirsch when he was the artistic director of the Stratford Festival. But in 1985, he had given up on Canada.

When I went to see him, he was directing a play on Broadway, a movie in Hollywood, and he was teaching at Yale.

"The problem with Canadian culture is neither the markets nor its geography," he told me. "There's something fundamentally missing from our chromosomal makeup." Hirsch emigrated from Hungary to Canada after losing most of his family in the Holocaust. He was grateful to Winnipeg for helping him to launch a very successful career, and he had come to love the promise of Canada. Now living in the U.S., he no longer had any faith that English Canadians would ever really become a people, with a unique identity. According to Hirsch, they lacked the desire to become themselves.

"Some people have the desire and others don't. And some nations have it and others don't. I don't know whose fault that is. Maybe God never intended Canadians to be Canadians. Or maybe he put us down next to the Americans to test us and we failed the test. We just don't have the stuff."

What Hirsch suspected was that, while we might escape actual U.S. occupation, our imaginations were being conquered by the Americans. "I think if most Canadians were to wake up tomorrow and be part of the U.S., they would just go to work and say, oh! We'll have cheaper vegetables. And the price of cars will be cheaper. Hooray!"

"Do you think that's inevitable?

"I think it's inevitable that the distinction will disappear in a hundred years, yes."

We have a chance for the first time to bring up a generation that is not cultural cripples and parasites. Who don't have the word dull flash in their skull whenever the word Canada is heard. We could bring up a generation of Canadians who know and like and respect ourselves. If we don't do it in this generation, it's not going to be done at all. The biggest struggle for small nations is to survive . . . Look at a map of the turn of the century. Countries, like people, have lifespans.

Canada will not always be here. We don't have forever to make our statement. To light our flame.

John Gray

John MacLachlan Gray is best known for *Billy Bishop Goes to War*, a play that's been staged all over Canada and the United States, winning multiple awards. But in 1985, his speech in Kitchener was a call to arms for Canadians. When I first heard it, I hoped it would help people understand the threats we faced and that they would care enough to hold on to what we had. I don't think that they did, and our failure to adequately resist in 1985 is directly tied to the crisis we face in 2025.

Much of the material in this essay was in a CBC *Ideas* series I produced forty years ago. When a version of the program was rebroadcast in early 2025, a number of listeners told me that hearing Gray's speech again brought back that time in the 1980s. They remembered the sense of peril so many of us felt, along with the deep and abiding desire to stop being moths buzzing around the American flame—to finally become a fully sovereign nation.

The Canada–U.S. Free Trade Agreement expanded in the 1990s to include Mexico and life just went on. We got cheaper vegetables and cars, houses in Florida, a vast market for our steel and wood. We failed to notice that we were growing dependent on the U.S. until Donald Trump threatened to cut us off. We had been lulled into a sense of prosperity, and we stopped caring about what we were losing. Until Trump announced that our entire existence as a nation was simply an arbitrary line drawn on a map and that, on a whim, he could erase it.

Donald Trump has stirred us from our lotus-induced stupor. Something has happened in Canada that I haven't seen before: a rejection of that unhealthy dependence, a will to nationhood, a generation that wants to light its own flame. I'm seeing an energy and self-assurance that was only present as a sketch, a vague outline, in 1985. The rallies of today are positive, youthful, and determined.

My son is now forty-eight, with children of his own, all of them fiercely Canadian and comfortable in their own skins. In so many ways, we have matured as a country. We are telling our own stories to each other, even if we don't always have a place to put them or the money to compete with the American juggernaut. We are a very different country today than in 1985—and, even though most people living in Canada can see the United States on a clear day, we have managed to remain a very different place.

We face formidable odds. Most of our newspapers are now owned by American hedge funds; the television that many Canadians watch is from U.S. streaming services; Silicon Valley has colonized our minds through social media; we turn to Google for just about every question that we have; Hollywood still controls our cinemas; and foreign companies own our publishing industry. And yet—somehow—we find ourselves deeply attached to this idea of Canada: an entity not quite defined, but a country whose moment to shine has certainly arrived.

A few years after I last saw him, John Hirsch returned to Canada. He died in Toronto in 1989 of AIDS-related illnesses. I am sorry that he never got to see his adopted country find its voice. He would have enjoyed this chapter.

Manifesting More Than Elbows Up

During his inauguration speech on January 20, 2025, new U.S. president Donald Trump used a phrase that chilled the soul.

"We will pursue our Manifest Destiny into the stars," he said, "launching American astronauts to plant the Stars and Stripes on the planet Mars."

Trump may have been alluding to a future in outer space, but he was really talking about the past on this continent. "Manifest Destiny" is a term coined by American writer John L. O'Sullivan in 1845, expressing the longstanding and racist belief that the United States is culturally, religiously, and socially superior to all; a nation chosen by God to inherit the earth—and now, apparently, the universe. The primary motivation of evoking Manifest Destiny, of course, is to make the argument that any and all opposed to U.S. hegemony and dominance are enemies—so it should come as little surprise that the idea instigated the public to support the displacement and genocide of Indigenous peoples; a practice that has never really stopped. Full of principles birthed in the Doctrine of Discovery and European imperialism, Manifest Destiny is a code word calling for conquest, invasion, and violence.

Trump now wants to make American imperialism great again. His playbook is to position himself as God's emissary— something he also did during his inauguration speech, when he referred to the unsuccessful assassination attempt on his life during the 2024 election campaign as a moment he was "saved by God to make America great again." This time, though, the mission to spread American dominance is not to Mars but to the north: turning Canada into the 51st state— whether Canadians want it or not.

Welcome to Indigenous life, Canada. You now get a taste of what it's like to have one's culture attacked, leadership demeaned, and economy undermined. Up next will be land invasion, resource exploitation, and the introduction of dra-conian systems that implement pain and suffering. Then, when resistance and fighting back becomes the only option, the final step of this process emerges when one is blamed for an oppressor's selfishness, paternalism, and aggression. Welcome to the struggle, my Canadian relations.

Here's the good news: Canadians can learn a lot from Indigenous nations about how Manifest Destiny takes place, feels, and what happens afterwards. Here's the bad news: things get bad—indeed, very bad—before they get better. The fight against Manifest Destiny requires one to battle a lot of very bad—even nonsensical—ideas full of righteousness, lies, and arrogance. There's also a need to define one's priori-ties, crystallize goals, and make very hard decisions with not a lot of time. And, most of all, the fight against invasion must always be a brave one, for the power of fear, apathy, and self-ishness is alluring.

If there's anything to thank Trump for, it is his blatant, blunt commitment to himself. Indigenous peoples know this spirit well; having not only dealt with it in leaders who arrived in our communities but within ourselves. If there is any teaching Indigenous cultures and communities understand, it is that we live in a harsh and demanding world that requires cooperation, collectivity, and compromise to survive and thrive. Colonialism is hard, but the winter, mosquitoes, and hunger are far harder and demand more to overcome. All of us have stories of what happens when we turn away from the teachings of community and care, and prioritize individuality, competitiveness, and material accumulation. Amongst the Anishinaabe, my culture, the centrality of these values results in the arrival of the Wiindigo, a huge cannibalistic spirit that feeds on fear and emerges during deadly forces like winter or starvation. In his 1995 book *Manitous: The Spiritual World of the Ojibway*, Anishinaabe theorist and storyteller Basil Johnston described this being as a monster who:

> towered five to eight times above the height of a tall man . . . Because it was afflicted with never-ending hunger and could never get enough to eat, it was always on the verge of starvation. The Weendigo was gaunt to the point of emaciation, its desiccated skin pulling tautly over its bones . . . As the Weendigo ate, it grew, and as it grew so did its hunger, so that no matter how much it ate, its hunger always remained in proportion to its size.

The comparison between Trump and the Wiindigo of course is unfair; Trump is not that tall. He does have gaunt, orange skin though, and an insatiable hunger for McDonald's. In other words, a Wiindigo comes in many forms, even a U.S. president, but lives off the power that comes when people turn on one another, build walls, and believe lies instead of facts.

It is ironic that in response to Trump's threats against Canadian sovereignty, Canadians turned to the question: *who are we?* Insert commercial featuring comedian Mike Myers here. The existential question of what is Canada is time-honoured, and more, of course, than just national pride, the flag, and the hockey term "elbows up"—but this phrase articulates well the determination Canadians feel when faced with Trump's threats. "Elbows up" offers Canadians the idea best manifested during Team Canada's struggles against Team USA in the NHL's 4 Nations tournament: the fight for what Canada hopes, believes, and imagines itself to be. The platform of hockey—a sport all about the struggle for territory and penetration into the last remaining place another community protects—is perfect in this scenario, for Canadians need to articulate their most core values in order to protect the opposition from scoring their goal.

For decades—particularly since the flag was used by anti-vaccination advocates during the COVID-19 pandemic—Canadian identity has been uncomfortable to talk about. Seen best during a professional hockey tournament win, Trump has changed that conversation. Now, conversations on what make Canada special are back in style, but demand more if one doesn't want to repeat the mistakes, harms, and problems of the past. For instance, if one asked the typical Canadian what makes Canada unique, one undoubtedly hears: the land, politeness, empathy, and freedom—all of which have various manifestations found in the economy, democracy, social welfare system and healthcare, and multiculturalism. These are worthy and important things foundational to the Canadian identity—but all were also invented by Indigenous peoples. Understanding this fact is not only the most important step this country needs to take, but may be how the notion of the 51st state is stopped.

Every single thing that is Canadian begins with Indigenous contributions. This is obvious when it comes to the land, the economy, and even the flag (who showed Europeans the importance of maple trees?), but is perhaps less known when it comes to everything else. So, simple questions are in order: Who do you think introduced the concept that citizens can disagree but come together to create peaceful institutions that make decisions for the whole? Who do you think came up with the idea that community members can share wealth by collecting a portion of their food, medicine, and time, and distributing them, feeding, and healing the most disenfranchised, sick, and poor first? Who do you think introduced the concept of multiculturalism, the idea that newcomers are permitted—even encouraged—to maintain their original cultures while joining a larger nation? Was it Europeans, who followed the orders of the church and the monarch while believing those who worshipped or lived differently were satanic savages? Or did Indigenous civilizations, who responded to harsh climates and landscapes by building functional, interdependent, and mutually beneficial relationships with everyone around them, and then taught these methods to their new relations—who they invited into treaty and building a country together? None of this, of course, takes away from the essential and unique things Canadians contributed as well—for it's all a mix built on a foundation.

In his victory speech after winning a minority government during the 2025 federal election, Canadian prime minister Mark Carney said:

> As I've been warned, America wants our land, our resources, our water, our country. But these are not idle threats. President Trump is trying to break us so that America can own us. That will never, that will never ever happen . . .
>
> Canada is more than a nation. We are and we always will be a confederation. A sacred set of ideas and ideals built on practical foundations that we know were not always perfect, but we always strive to be good. We do things because they're right, not because they're easy and we see kindness as a virtue, not as a weakness. Most importantly, we know that our strength lies in our resolve to work together as a country. It relies on our unity . . .
>
> We become just by doing just acts, brave by doing brave acts. When we are kind, kindness grows. When we seek unity, unity grows. When we are Canadian, Canada grows. And united, [in] our history, we have done hard, seemingly impossible things. United, we have built one nation in harsh conditions, despite a sometimes hostile neighbour. Yes, they have form on this, the Americans. United, we have confronted our

own past with Indigenous peoples. United, we have created universal public health care. And now, in the face of this crisis, united, we are buying Canadian. We are exploring everything this country has to offer.

Canada's imperfect and "practical foundation" based in "kindness as a virtue, not as a weakness" is living proof that this country's central core principles are, and always have been, Indigenous. This unity is forged through "impossible things" that begin with love, respect, honesty, bravery, truth, humility, and wisdom; kind acts demonstrated by introducing new-comers to this place, teaching them where the medicine and the food can be found, and bringing settlers into our lodges, longhouses, and ᐃᒡᓗᐃᑦ (igluit) so they can join with us to build a place where we all can live safely, securely, and collectively.

Canadians eternally struggle with the existential questions of what does this country mean, where is it going, and why is it here? The anxiety surrounding the answers to these questions becomes polarized in the face of Trump. This uncertainty is in large part because Indigenous contributions are mis-understood, bastardized, or simply absent in most areas of the country. With due respect to Carney, Canada hasn't com-pletely "confronted" the fact this country declared war upon the very people who gave Canadians every single thing that makes them who they are. During a long nation-building project obsessed with Wiindigos—encouraging Canadians to dominate the land, stop at nothing to build the economy, and centralize competitiveness, capitalism, and individuality—Canada left behind Indigenous communities, and it continues to do so today. So, it is ironic that, when a country is confronted with a larger, more threatening Wiindigo, it turns away from selfishness and toward collectivity as an antidote. It's as if everyone in this country suddenly put on the same coloured shirt that said "Every One Matters" and marched. I wonder who came up with that?

The problem, of course, is that simply building pipelines and houses, cutting taxes, and "buying Canadian" will not be enough to battle Trump's threats of American imperialism. Simply put, one cannot "build, baby, build" without "reconcile, baby, reconcile." We must turn to what makes us believe that the person beside each of us matters—a principle that must find its way into how we vote, build an economy, and help and heal one another. Stating empty territorial acknowledgements is never going to cut it; Canadian sovereignty relies on relationships with Indigenous peoples via treaties, Indigenous rights, and a complicated array of laws that include Indigenous and treaty rights at their centre. Simply put, Canada must learn its own history and follow its own laws, putting Indigenous peoples at the centre of any and all conversations surrounding Canada's future. The good news is that, as in every single step of this country, Indigenous peoples will continue to be willing partners for Canadians to help this process, as our cultures, teachings, and futures demand us to be.

An immense part of this process emerged during the 2025 federal election campaign, when a record twelve Indigenous MPs were elected by Canadians. Primarily elected on the prairies—where a cognizance of Indigenous-Canadian relationships comes from proportional populations and everyday interactions—this led to a record three Indigenous peoples in cabinet. Two of these appointments were Mandy Gull-Masty

(Cree) as Indigenous Services minister, and Rebecca Chartrand (Anishinaabe, Ininew, Métis) as Northern and Arctic Affairs minister and minister responsible for the Canadian Northern Economic Development Agency. Indigenous women—historically Canada's most mistreated group—are now in charge of arguably two of the most critical segments of Carney's plan to build infrastructure, develop critical minerals and resources, and fortify Canadian sovereignty. Imagine this now: if business leaders want to develop the land or initiate oil and gas projects, or if Vladimir Putin or Trump want to come knocking on Canada's North—they will have to talk to an Indigenous woman.

That's a little more than elbows up.

CATHERINE LEROUX
Translation by Mélissa Bull

Will: A Short Story

Don Will was a retired philosopher—if anyone ever really retires from philosophy. From his terrace in Tegucigalpa, he could see my country far more clearly than I, still in my twenties, could. "French," he said one evening, "is what prevents Canada from dissolving into the United States." I'd wondered whether this was wisdom or the fancies of a Franco-Caribbean man bearing an Irish name. Twenty-five years later, I understood the possibilities his sentence carried.

The day after the annexation, the president banned the use of French. Indigenous and immigrant languages soon followed. We weren't surprised—he had, after all, homed in on Spanish and inclusive language from the first days of his endless second reign, long before his takeover of Canada. Schools, the media, and the courts were now conducted exclusively in English—if you could call this twisted language, stripped of every possibility of truth, English. Everything that was said and written in the public sphere rang as if trapped within a hollow, plasticized shell, suffocating reality. The anglophile in me was sorry. The francophone woman was up in arms. I wasn't the only one.

Over whispered conversations, drowned out by Sinatra hits we blasted at top volume, we began to organize. There were only seven of us at first, then, quickly, there were twenty, one hundred. We named our group "Will." A syllable embodying future and volition in English, and which contains the sound of the French "yes," *oui*. That's what we repeated, *oui*, at every meeting. Our resistance was acquiescence—to risk, to fear, to imagination.

From our first meeting in the basement of a derelict library, Tom reminded us that his mother tongue had once helped relay military secrets. During the First World War, Cree code talkers had outsmarted the most seasoned German cryptologists. From there grew the idea of communicating via dissident languages. Tremblay's Joual mixed with Daigle's Chiac, crossed with Bacon's Innu-aimun, coupled with Patsauq's Inuktitut. The mixtures of French, Creole, and Arabic that sprouted from the linguistic incubators of Montreal and Laval schoolyards. The dialects of the old Italians of Petite-Patrie and the Vietic accents of the third-generation Vietnamese communities. As our networks branched out, the amalgamation spread, from Ukrainian and Prairie Michif to Hakka and the Salish languages of the West Coast. Our actions were discussed from coast to coast to coast, thanks to not one, but dozens of covert codes.

We planted bombs, destroyed symbols. We hacked platforms, published manifestos. We sabotaged facilities, paralyzed systems. We plastered our cities' walls with messages of resistance in every language. The grey shadow of the occupation continued to expand. Arbitrary closures, layoffs, and internments intensified. Several of us were wiretapped.

We were many; we contained millions of words, but it wasn't enough. We didn't have the right weapons.

One night, Sarah showed up brandishing a half-decomposed science fiction novel. The relic from her distant CEGEP studies had slipped behind her bookcase. In the novel, the characters' language was so precise and synthetic that it became a weapon—a power capable of transmogrifying matter. "*This* is what we have to do," she said. I didn't see how it could work. But the others did. They were word people. Nurses who'd saved lives with a kind remark, elders who'd saved kindred with a legend. They were teachers, saleswomen, sweet talkers, telephone operators, inventors, travellers. They were all poets. They knew that a word could shake the earth. "This is possible," they said.

We got to work, searching for ways to reduce language to its most simple, most extreme expression. We had *Dune* in mind: "My name is a killing word." Since we were living in a dystopia, we had to use science fiction to reason. We tried syncretisms, neologisms, magical incantations. We isolated radicals, we agglutinated performative morphemes. I thought of nothing else, carrying our impossible syllables with me everywhere I went—in the streets, on the subways patrolled by soldiers, at home with the lights out. I mumbled words overcrowded with consonants under my employers' scrutinizing eyes. Sometimes I'd catch one of them shiver for no reason. I smiled inwardly.

Mobilized by this project, Will slowed its operations. The explosions ceased, as did the ransacking of the occupiers' computer networks. They thought they'd succeeded in crushing us. The unilingual president and his horde of unilingual sycophants couldn't imagine what was at work in a mind where syntaxes and lexicons imbricated, rending universes. It wasn't the bombs that threatened their monomaniacal regime, but the ebullience of languages that had survived, proliferating like underground mycelia.

It took months. We read and reread Sarah's novel, as well as other books that had escaped the shredders. We grew discouraged; we persisted. *Oui. Will.* And then, one night, Tom whispered the word, a hybrid of all known language families, and we felt the air vibrate around us. We knew at once that we shouldn't speak it aloud, not until the appointed time. We caught it, hid it between our teeth, inscribed it within us. I mouth it several times a day, like an explosive diction exercise. I sleep between its phonemes, protected by its roots.

Tomorrow, when I start my service at the governor's office, when the president arrives with his skittish and bloated lackeys, when I test the microphone before his speech, I won't say, "One, two." I will speak with a strong, multifaceted voice that holds entire nations. I will pronounce our word—a single, ballistic word—and the earth will tremble.

Who We Really Are

There are some patterns you see over and over when you're a doctor, and here is one that endures: when a person is facing an unexpected crisis, they land very quickly on what matters most.

Sometimes people do splinter into fragments, at least at first. The betrayal of something they took for granted—a heart that always pumped, a perfectly agreeable limb that followed commands, an organ they barely even knew was there because it was such a good citizen—goes off like a little bomb. And there they are, cowering in the middle of what's left, scarcely able to believe their eyes, their ears, their new reality. But that doesn't usually last long, because for all our faults and blind spots as a species, we are phenomenally adaptive. We reconfigure—goals, plans, relationships. Things fall away, like shedding skin. And underneath that skin is something a little bit extraordinary: who we really are.

Ask a Canadian who *they* think they are and you will get 40 million different answers. Mine weaves in geography, history, and hand puppets. I was born in 1974, about sixty miles from the U.S. border between Manitoba and North Dakota.

My dad spent time in the air force; my mom once worked for the CBC. I was chaperoned through early childhood by Mr. Dressup, Casey, and Finnegan. I loved Gordon Lightfoot and Anne Murray. I thought Barbara Frum was an icon, Terry Fox a legend. I sang "God Save the Queen" and "O Canada" at every school assembly, belting out the words as if I were on stage at Roy Thomson Hall. I had a grandfather who fought in the First World War, and even though he died before I was born, every Remembrance Day when we chanted "In Flanders Fields" in our sombre, childish voices, I felt proud of his sacrifice.

Over the ensuing years, my understanding of Canadian identity became messier, more complex. Sometimes questions outnumbered answers. I grew up with two profoundly disabled siblings, and for them, this country was not a land of much opportunity. I was never taught the truth about residential schools; it wasn't until I was a practising physician that I realized I didn't know anything meaningful about the experiences of Indigenous peoples in Canada. Then, during the COVID-19 crisis, I watched as a convoy of massive trucks—subsidized heavily by a certain southern neighbour—occupied and paralyzed our nation's capital; crowds screamed that we were living under a dictatorship, their actions supported enthusiastically by the leader of an opposition party who hailed them as heroes. *Heroes.* I couldn't equate that word with any crowd of men and women shouting expletives, swearing and soaking in hot tubs on the streets of Ottawa, defiling the National War Memorial and the Tomb of the Unknown Soldier.

I thought of my grandfather . . . his lungs ruined by mustard gas, the invisible injuries he came home with that were even worse. I thought of hundred-year-old letters my dad had shown me throughout the years—one from his great-uncle, Chris, pleading to be allowed to enlist at the age of sixteen "like all the rest"; another a response to my great-grandfather, gently informing him that despite his request for special consideration, he could not be assigned active duty because he was older than the cut-off age of forty-eight.

Sometimes it felt like those letters came from more than another time—like they were from another *country*.

My dad once told me that my grandfather only ever spoke about the war on a single occasion. They were watching *All Quiet on the Western Front*—the 1930 Oscar-winning movie that portrays the physical and psychological cost of war for a group of young soldiers. About forty minutes into the movie, the men are stationed in the trenches. The enemy advances, and both sides kill each other by the thousands—screaming, stabbing, bayonetting, shooting, slaughtering en masse.

My grandfather said quietly, "That's exactly what it was like."

Somewhere, years ago, I read an interview with a historian. They said fascism will often resurface in societies only when the last people who fought or lived under a previous fascist regime have died. That's because memory is vivid, pulsatile, communicable. The living hold us accountable. "In Flanders Fields" and *All Quiet on the Western Front* can only do so much heavy lifting when the people who can tell us *that's exactly what it was like* are no longer here to warn us.

I felt privately that things might be hopeless. I wondered if my grandfather ever worried that his sacrifice would turn out to be for nothing, that it would only buy us time until the memories ran out.

———

But then came the unexpected, miraculous turn—acts of verbal and economic aggression from the United States rousing the sleeping emotions of millions of Canadians, an old, wartime brand of patriotism suddenly coming back to life. Flags on lawns and in windows, reclaimed from the convoy. A meme of Casey and Finnegan as the new Fentanyl Czars. Crowds at hockey games tearing up and going wild as the national anthem was performed at centre ice. An election with a near-record turnout. A *cri de cœur* in two official languages that reminded us we are part of something bigger than ourselves, and that something is not "O Canada."

It is *our* Canada.

We are a nation like almost every other—built on violence, cruelty, oppression, as well as ingenuity, hard work, tenacity, community, faith, hope, and the sacrifices of those who came before us. But that is only one truth about us . . . a puzzle piece, not the whole story. That story has taken a turn at just the right moment. Sometimes saying what you will never become— whether that is a fascist state or the 51st—is the thing that brings the most clarity.

My own father will be ninety this fall. He remembers what it was like to watch men go away to war. He remembers the terrible price men and women paid to subsidize our way of life. He talks about these stories. In February, we watched one of Justin Trudeau's press conferences together, sitting in front of the television just the way he once sat with his own father watching *All Quiet on the Western Front*. We listened to our prime minister remind us that we are not Americans, that the times ahead will be difficult, that our identity—whatever it is, whoever we are—is precious and worth fighting for.

We aren't facing the same kind of choices or sacrifices as my grandfather did. Not yet, anyway. But it was clear to us then, and it is every bit as true as I write this now—we are in a moment of alchemy, of transformation.

My dad, always a purveyor of wisdom, observed that there was one good thing in all of it.

"I think it woke us up a little," he said.

That is the essential truth—and it's exactly what this moment is like. Shedding a skin, bridging two worlds, awakening to the sacrifices of ancestors who made our way of life possible. Relearning lessons we once knew but had almost forgotten. Remembering, before our collective memory can fail us—maybe even just in the nick of time—who we really are.

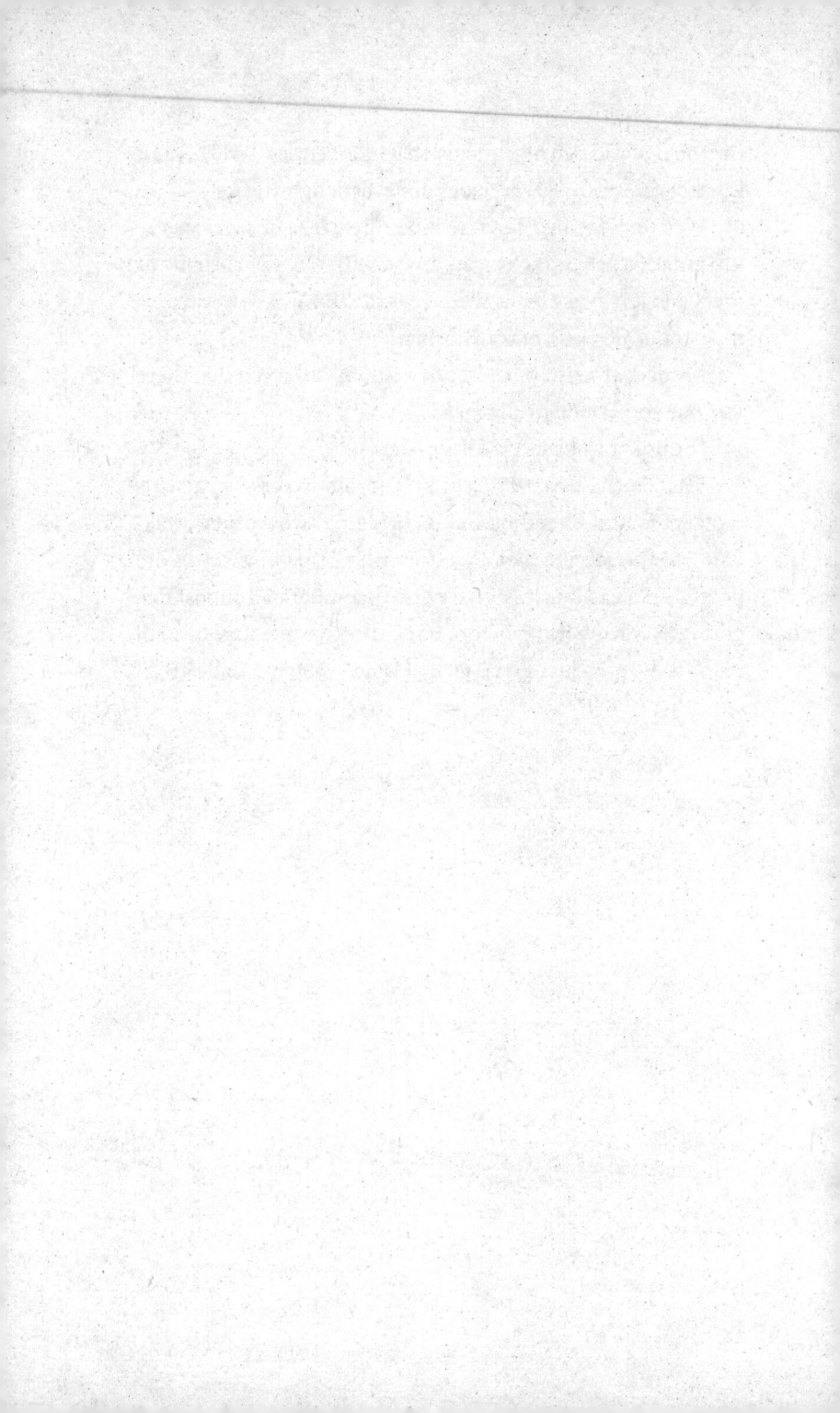

MARGARET LAURENCE
The New Romans (1968)

Open Letter to the Mother of Joe Bass

I don't know what you look like. We will not meet. I don't know
how old you are. About my age, I would guess, which is forty-
one. I don't know how many kids you have. I have two. My
daughter is fifteen, and my son is twelve. You have a twelve-
year-old son also.

My son was born in Ghana, and there was no doctor
present. The doctor was overworked, and I was okay and
normal, so there was only a midwife in attendance. She was
a Ghanaian, a matriarch, four kids of her own, and no male
doctor could have known what she knew. "It will be a boy," she
promised to me as the hours passed by. "Only a man could be
so stubborn." When I was in pain, she put out her hands to me
and let me clench them, and I held to those hands as though
they were my hope of life. "It will soon be over," she said.
"Would I lie to you? Look, I know. I have borne." She did
know. l had no anaesthetic, and when she delivered him, she
laid him, damp and thin and blood-smeared, across my belly.
"There," she said. "What did I tell you? Your boy, he is here."

She was the only other person present when I looked over God's shoulder at the birth of my son. She had had her children too, and she knew what it was that was happening. She knew that it had to be felt in the flesh to be really known.

In twelve years, so far, touch wood, my son has been lucky. Once in Africa he had malaria, and a few other times, in Canada and England, he had such things as throat infections or chicken pox. Each time I have been afraid in that one-way, guts of ice feeling that I could probably face anything at all except that something really bad should happen to one of my kids.

Now he rides on his bike for countless miles around the countryside. He is a science man at heart, and his electric train set has complicated switches and intricate wiring which he has rigged up himself and which miraculously work and make the miniature engines do as he bids. He has lived life so far among people who were basically friendly towards him. This is not to say that he has never felt pain. He has. More, even, than I know, and I know some of it. But at least until this point in his life, his pain has been something which he could, in some way, deal with by himself.

I have seen your son only once, Mrs. Bass. That was in a newspaper photograph. In Detroit, he went out one evening when his playmates asked him to. It was not an evening to be out. Your son was shot by the police. By accident, the paper said. Shot by accident in the neck. The police were aiming at Billy Furr, who was walking out of Mack Liquors, not with a fortune in his hands but with precisely six tins of stolen beer. When Billy Furr saw the police, something told him to run and keep on running, so he did that, and he was shot dead. But the police had fired more than once, and Joe Bass happened to be in the way. The papers did not say whether he was expected to recover or not, nor how much a twelve-year-old could recover from something like that. A Negro twelve-year-old.

Your son looked a skinny kid, a little taller than my twelve-year-old but not as robust. He was lying on the sidewalk, and his eyes were open. He was seeing everything, I guess, including himself. He was bleeding, and one of his hands lay languidly outstretched in a spillage of blood. His face didn't have any expression at all. I looked at the picture for quite a long time. Then I put it away, but it would not be put away. The blank kid-face there kept fluctuating in my mind. Sometimes it was the face of your son, sometimes of mine.

Then I recalled another newspaper photograph. It was of a North Vietnamese woman. Some marvelous new kind of napalm had just come into use. I do not understand the technicalities. This substance when it alights flaming onto skin cannot be removed. It adheres. The woman was holding a child who looked about eighteen months old, and she was trying to pluck something away from the burn-blackening area on the child's face. I wondered how she felt when her child newly took on life and emerged, and if she had almost imagined she was looking over God's shoulder then.

Mrs. Bass, these are the two pictures. I know they are not fair. I know the many-sidedness of that country in which you live. I know the people I love there, who are more heartbroken than I at the descent into lunacy. Also, I am a North American— I cannot exclude myself from the dilemma. I cannot say *them*. It is forced upon me to say *us*. Perhaps you know who the enemy is—and perhaps it is I.

Once, a long time ago, from the eyes of twenty-two, I wrote a poem about my father, or maybe about the local cemetery, in which the words said, *Under the stone lies my father, ten years dead, who would never know as his, this bastard world he sired*. It did not occur to me then that I would one day stand in that same relation to the world—no longer as a child, but as a parent.

I am not even sure who is responsible. Responsibility seems to have become too diffuse, and a whole continent (if not, indeed, a whole world) appears to be spinning in automation. The wheels turn, but no one admits to turning them. People with actual names and places of belonging are killed, and there is increasingly little difference between these acts and the fake deaths of the cowboys who never were. The fantasy is taking over, like the strangler vines of the jungle taking over the trees. It is all happening on TV.

Except that it isn't. You know, because you felt the pain in your own flesh, that evening when the police shot your son. Is it necessary to feel pain in our own flesh before we really know? More and more, I think that it probably is.

I have spent fifteen years of my life writing novels and other things. I have had, if any faith at all, a faith in the word. *In the beginning was the Word, and the Word was with God, and the Word was God*. The kind of belief that many writers have—the belief that if we are to make ourselves known to one another, if we are really to know the reality of another, we must communicate with what is almost the only means we have—human speech. There are other means of communication, I know, but they are limited because they are so personal and individual—we can make love; we can hold and comfort our children. Otherwise, we are stuck with words. We have to try to talk to one another, because the imperfect means is the only general one we have.

And yet—I look at the picture of your twelve-year-old son on the sidewalks of Detroit, pillowed in blood. And I wonder— if it were in physical fact *my* son, of the same age, would I be able to go on writing novels, in the belief that this was a worthwhile thing to be doing this year (as they say) of Our Lord? Mrs. Bass, I do not think I can answer that question.

I am afraid for all our children.

Too Wide to See and
Too Long to Know

In the depths of February—especially this past one, when snow fell in record clumps across my city, Toronto—we take whatever we can get to make us feel alive in the world, cocooned by couch throws and Netflix, waiting for the light to return. So when the National Hockey League first announced a novel four-team international contest to supplant the traditional by-rote all-star competition, it seemed mostly a bridge to get us through to spring—something to watch out of one eye between the dark hours. Besides, nation vs. nation men's hockey had, for a generation of wanting young fans, only been celebrated by parents and mature siblings old enough to have watched Sidney Crosby feather the puck between Ryan Miller's pads in Vancouver, or Mario Lemieux torch the Russians in Hamilton in 1987, or—in the Mesozoic age—Paul Henderson score three straight winning goals in the last three games of the first Summit Series in Moscow. Recent times had seen NHL commissioner Gary Bettman demure on global play, withdrawing the best of the men's pros until certain demands—insurance, rebroadcasting rights—were met by the IIHF. As a result, neither Connor McDavid nor Auston Matthews nor Victor Hedman had the opportunity to measure their genius against one another on the international stage, bereft in a time of administrative chess play.

Snow fell and temperatures sank. Frank and I —my Italo-Canadian neighbour with whom I share the distinction of us having bought, and moved into, our Italo-Canadian grand-parents' homes within a few years of each other—woke most mornings to the squealing of car tires fighting to get out of iced-in parking spots, the two of us emerging collars-high with gloves, shovels, and planks of wood to free stranded Acuras and Hyundais. Walking around the neighbourhood that win-ter after a tromp to the corner store inevitably meant being consumed by gusts of flurries, new layers of snow painting the ground whenever it threatened to go the way of grey slush. The evenings grew darker faster and streetlamps glowed against the cruel sky. After dinner, I would step sweater'ed into my glerups and lie back across the couch, searching for the remote between cushions.

The NHL had paused their season for a two-week break, and while most of the players left dressing rooms flip-flopped for languid days on beaches and yachts, the best ninety or so skaters in the world—minus Putin's Russians as well as the Czechs, Slovaks, Germans, and Swiss—headed to their respective national team camps, fitting in just two designated training days before the real thing started. In normal times, the tournament would have built slowly—some slow chords over a gentle snare and maybe the murmur of a voice, before going full "Who's Next" by the time the final between the two best teams came around—but, because it was a short event, and because the Americans had re-elected Donald Trump, the 4 Nations suddenly became heavy with must-win games alongside everything the American president, and therefore America, now symbolized: antipathy, greed, aggression, misanthropy, and a callous sense of self-determination.

After his inauguration in January, Trump had opined about the possible annexation of Canada, repeatedly using the term *51st state* in press gatherings the way one might use the term *fixed mortgage*, as if continental invasions were merely transactional. Trump openly mocked Trudeau, the exiting PM, and told crowds that he viewed the border as an antiquated scribble, randomly drawn by a fool in a beard and briarwood pipe. American players—some of whom, like Matthews, Brady Tkachuk, and others who captained Canadian teams—were asked how they felt about their president wanting to eclipse Canada's sovereignty, and, having been programmed from an early age to speak in neutral, they expertly said nothing until they did not. Later in the tournament, Trump telephoned the American team in their dressing room—it became obvious early on that he was immune to the exact language of the game—and J.T. Miller, not being able to help himself, said that "it was awesome to get his support," despite the fact that crowds in the city where he had until recently played, Vancouver, had booed "The Star-Spangled Banner" to protest Trump's gentle threats, if there is such a thing.

In past times, especially during the Cold War, the Russians had routinely worn the black hat, and I can remember watching the 1972 Summit Series believing that, if Canada didn't emerge victorious, we might fall prey to communism, and our lives would change forever. In morning classes that fall, we watched 8mm movies on a projector wheeled in on a stand about what to do in case of a nuclear attack, while in the evening, CTV broadcast the Russia team taking apart the Canadians on the ice as they deadheaded their way across the country, before the event moved to the U.S.S.R. Later tourneys possessed less political drama—the world was changing, Russian players were defecting here, and Canada was sailing along unrivalled as the pre-eminent hockey nation—and even through the 1990s and 2000s, when Team USA began icing real stars with unassailable NHL pedigrees, there was never any sense that a loss to an opponent would mean a national crisis or humiliation at the hands of an adversary. But in 2025, and after years without serious men's international competitions, two things had changed: the American stars were now on par with the Canadians, and their wretched president was a monstrous dreamer who might one day consume us whole.

Despite being a public Canadian hockey person—player, author, filmmaker, and, once, playwright (of *The Five Hole Stories*)—I've tried to cheer Americans wherever possible, owing to fans I've met over the years who, because they love the game dearly, have a sense of Canada that's steeped in history, geography, and culture. During my first hockey journey abroad, I played in China with the Foxes of Peapack, New Jersey, who graciously absorbed me into the fold on their tour of Asia. The late Marc Nathan—who, among other things, was Seymour Stein's A&R bird dog, discovering the Barenaked Ladies and signing them to Sire—had an encyclopedic knowledge of the minor leagues—names, stats, trophies—and, as a gay man in California in the 1970s, befriended the wives of L.A. Kings players. He was with them the night Billy Harris Jr. was traded from Long Island. "They all wondered if he had a big cock," he told me. "They were excited that a new guy was coming in who they could fuck." Buffalo's Jeff Z. Klein, one of my literary mentors, was the sports editor for *The Village Voice*, and his early columns about the Rangers showed me what kind of writer I wanted to be. Other Americans—like Stu Hackel, who ran NHL media from New York, Art Berglund, and Brooklyn's Lou Vairo, an early pioneer of USA Hockey— gave me hours of their time to talk about what it was like, as an American, to be an outsider in the Canadian game, some- thing I'd never considered. Their experience in hockey in the 1970s, '80s, and '90s wasn't that different from mine as an alternative musician trying to establish myself against the corporate-scape of Canadian music, or as a hockey writer wanting to tell stories from rinks in Harbin or Hong Kong instead of the Corel Centre. For years, people had a jaundiced view of southern hockey culture, and Americans had to grind and, ultimately, win to be afforded any kind of respect, although their "Miracle on Ice" triumph in 1980 was consid- ered by some Canadians to be the result of Soviet hubris rather than American talent.

No matter how intensely political it got during 4 Nations, and no matter how brusquely the president tried to impose himself on the event the way he tried to impose himself on everything else, I reminded myself that some American cele- brations would be pure, and a good thing would happen to good people, no matter how hard I hoped against it.

———

Over Family Day weekend, the Canadians played the Americans in the round robin, losing 3–1 and ceding top spot to the U.S. After the game, J.T. Miller—again, not helping himself—revealed that the Americans had hatched an outrageous plan over an evening's group text: a few players would fling their gloves away and fight the Canadians the moment the puck hit the ice. This happened. There were three scraps in the first nine seconds. In a vacuum, men slugging at each other is not the kind of thing anyone needs to see—premeditated brawls possess none of the passion and fervour that more tempestuous fights do—but in a charged political setting where one team's head of state had told the other's that his country should not exist as a nation (all of this in a time of war in Gaza and Ukraine), I found myself rising from my couch to make sure what I was seeing was real, my heart pounding through my shirt.

Brady and Matthew, the Tkachuk brothers—more classically, and brashly, American than, say, Mike Modanos who predated them, and outrageously rendered as if by a *Mad* magazine cartoonist imagining what an off-the-hook hockey player should look like to an eleven-year-old—circled their combatants while chewing the mouth guard like a horse's bit before wildly swinging at Brandon Hagel and Sam Bennett, both of whom showed an alarming amount of poise considering the surprise assault. In the following shift, Miller came at defenceman Colton Parayko in the crease, engaging in the third bout and looking less like a middleweight trying to get on the inside than a petulant ape batting at fruit flies. Still, everything about the nature of our continent was manifest in that hot moment, with Matthews, Mexico's proxy, watching from the bench. It was visceral, ugly, and astonishing. Coming off the ice into the penalty box, the Tkachuks brayed at the Bell Centre crowd, applauding themselves and each other. The Americans had dragged the game by its heels into the ditch, and won. That Team Canada had let them said as much about our play as it did theirs.

While it's hard to celebrate hockey's cultural and societal glue without sounding like an apologist for a game troubled by abusive climates, an anti-LGBTQ agenda (in 2023, the NHL suspended any Pride imagery from its games), and an elite white athletic body, the game can still comfort us like an old cottage blanket, even when that blanket is set on fire—which is something you could imagine Matthew Tkachuk doing, slipping downstairs in his nightdress and cap with a Bic lighter tucked into the band of his underpants. Reels of the game's fights were everywhere. J.T. Miller said it "was the coolest experience I've probably had on the ice," which probably says more about how few trophies he's won than he'd like. Hagel, for his part, said "we're out there playing for the flag, not the cameras," and when asked about group chats, confessed that his team didn't have one, which led Matthew to suggest that Team Canada couldn't like each other very much. Narrative lather grew as the press converged to cover the rematch, and media experts predicated, correctly, that the championship would be the most-watched hockey game in U.S. history (nine million people tuned in).

On the evening of the game, I walked five kilometres in my long dark winter coat through the city to my friend's shed—the gathering point for our longstanding men's hockey team—as if spending time moving in the cold was a rite that this kind of game had earned. On my route I passed the frosted window of Empire Falafel on Bloor, whose Eritrean owner, Mohammed, was standing in front of the big screen at the back of the store, flicking past countless African and Arab league football matches to try to find the pregame broadcast. Earlier in the day, he'd laughed and told me he'd be tuning in to see Canada "give it to those bad guys down south," so I opened the door, bringing a swoosh of the cold breeze behind me, and shouted "22, channel 22," to him before ducking out. On the street, there were people everywhere in Leaf and Team Canada toques and scarves, striding below apartment windows with flags draped over them. A wave of nerves and sick excitement found me, before I remembered something that had happened in 2002 at the gold medal game in Salt Lake City—a match that would produce Canada's first men's gold in hockey in fifty years—when I telephoned my friend Brad Pascall, then head of communications with Hockey Canada. Answering the phone, he told me he was in the dressing room as the players were getting ready to play. "Mario Lemieux, Joe Sakic, they're right in front of me," he said. I asked him how they were, imagining them to be as ill and anxious as I was. Instead, he told me, "Dave, they're so excited. They can't wait to get going." It was a good reminder why I was writing about the game instead of playing in it.

The puck dropped a few moments after singer Chantal Kreviazuk bent the words to "O Canada" to sing "that only us command" at the frothy crowd in the sold-out Boston rink. Before the game, the Americans' GM, former Oiler Bill Guerin, had said he hoped that Trump would attend the final game, but he didn't, possibly choosing to tend to the business of running a nation, but just as possibly not. The game was smooth, lightning-fast, and as close as a whisper to an ear, running into overtime after Sam Bennett tied the score in the second period. Looking back, the Americans' behaviour in the round robin game was a lot like their president's, producing endless media heat yet ill-conceived, without a thought to what would follow. What the U.S. team had done could only be done once—any further aggression wouldn't have the impact it had arriving cold, out of the blue—and by the time the final began, the Canadians could play knowing that the U.S. had, literally, thrown their best punch. The teams settled into what mattered most—game play—with Canada relying on four key players: McDavid, the speed demon; forward Nate MacKinnon, who plays every shift like a person trying to bust through a facade; defenceman Cale Makar, the Fred Astaire of hockey; and resolute captain Sidney Crosby, who has never lost very much at anything. You could fit the darting, smart Leaf forward Mitch Marner in that group, too, although he's skated most of his career in the shadow of his Toronto teammate Auston Matthews, who in the 2024–25 season scored sixty-nine goals before being awarded team captaincy. In this game Marner expertly assisted on the tying and winning goals, the latter shunted to McDavid past a lunging Matthews, as if Marner had directly challenged his teammate's ability to intercept the puck, which he could not. The puck went in, the Canadians besieged goalie Jordan Binnington in a scrum of joy, and the Tkachuks hung their heads at the bench, mouth guards hidden in the depths of their gloves.

You could hear exultant cries of victory down Lukow Terrace behind the shed; and, in one instance, a friend told me he saw two sets of neighbours immediately run outside, as if having to tell someone else what they'd just seen. A small inconsequential chalice was produced on the ice, and the players twirled it in their arms for a moment. A bigger symbol was needed for everything the game, and games, had produced, but it would forever be too wide to see and too long to know, so we put on our boots and coats and headed back into the frozen winter's night.

Canadian Style

As a kid growing up in the 1960s, the grand allure of America was nothing short of intoxicating. Most family vacations were spent stateside, visiting aunts and uncles in Brooklyn—two of which owned toy stores. Being able to pop into their emporiums and have my pick of the latest dolls, like a "Betsy Wetsy," and gizmos, like a "Slinky," was exciting and empowering. Those trendy new toys, which were always first to debut in the States, made me the envy of all the neighbourhood kids back home. My Aunt Dora and Uncle Harry lived in Coney Island, walking distance to the amusement park. There was no doubt in my mind that the U.S.A. was fantasyland.

Then there were those fabulous second-hand clothes—castoffs from our well-heeled cousins Adrienne and Geraldine in Passaic, New Jersey. Every few months, another large box would arrive at our house, stuffed with high-quality "Made in America" garments that our cousins had outgrown or simply tired of. These pieces bore swish labels from upscale New York stores, and were more sophisticated and fashion-forward than anything we could ever dream of purchasing in Toronto.

My sister and I were wildly inspired by this chic, preloved clothing, and we cajoled our doting mum, who had recently purchased a new sewing machine, to new creative heights, as she painstakingly crafted original fashion fare for us that would measure up to the fancy old pieces our cousins had sent.

Regularly poring over the pages of American glossies like *Vogue* and *Harper's Bazaar* provided additional inspiration. But when it came time to shop for the latest trends, there was little or nothing in our local stores. The only place for mod-style pieces, outside of the U.K., seemed to be the States, and regular shopping trips to Buffalo were *de rigueur*. When the opportunity arose to take a family car trip to Florida in 1964, I was in heaven: I knew I'd be sure to find the go-go boots I was obsessing over in Miami. And I did! Once again, I was the envy of my neighbourhood pals.

Just when we were convinced that America was THE place to shop for fabulous fashion, my savvy sister discovered a chic little boutique in Toronto's Yorkville village called The Unicorn, run by Marilyn Brooks, an American-born designer who'd moved to Canada in the early 1960s. The Unicorn featured some of the coolest garb imaginable, and while we couldn't afford to splurge on too many of these fantastic pieces, just knowing that we could head down to Yorkville on a Saturday afternoon and swoon over the colourful racks of mod gear was a joy. Imagine! Such ultra-cool threads in our own backyard! Toronto had finally arrived on the fashion front, and suddenly all those Buffalo and Miami shopping sprees didn't seem necessary. A handful of groovy boutiques were springing up in the city, like Mr. Freedom on Yonge Street and Applestone Clothing Theatre on Avenue Road.

Finally, young Toronto fashionistas could find the forward, edgy fashion they were looking for.

When I moved to New York to study acting in the early 1970s, my personal style went through an interesting change. I was nineteen, and coming into my own—a budding actress who'd already met with some professional success and who was now acutely aware of her Canadian roots. Because I wasn't American, like everyone else in my class, I was somewhat of an exotic bird. Everyone seemed curious about life and the state of showbiz in Canada, and I couldn't be prouder to sing my country's praises. I began to realize that personal style had much more to do with authenticity than it had to do with the clothes on my back. I adopted an almost defiant fashion attitude: I wasn't compelled to dress in hot, sexy duds any longer. Riding the subways alone at night and strolling down city streets solo had started to feel a little intimidating. And I certainly didn't want to ask for attention. So I bought myself some baggy, denim men's overalls and a pair of construction boots, and instantly felt a lot more wholesome, down-to-earth, and oddly—and proudly—Canadian. I was making a style statement that went beyond the clothes. My new, unassuming look had more to do with the no-nonsense way I moved through the world than any of my sartorial trappings.

Throughout the 1970s, I became even more aware of my Canadian identity. After a couple of years of living in New York, I moved to Paris to continue my performance studies. As a mime-in-training, I became especially aware of the importance of body language. And while costume may help to tell personal stories, I learned that actions usually resonate more loudly. Again, I waved that Canadian flag proudly during my

Parisian sojourn. Most of the people I hung out with had never been to Canada, and it brought me great joy to tell them all I could about my home and native land. I was especially thrilled when I heard they were big Leonard Cohen fans! "Do you know he's Canadian?" I asked excitedly.

In 1975, I moved to St. John's, and it felt like the final frontier. What was this far-flung, enigmatic island all about? Working at CBC Radio as an arts producer, I quickly fell in love with the heart and soul of Newfoundland—its charming, unpretentious nature and salt-of-the-earth people. This perhaps was Canada at its best. Inspired by the crafty friends I'd made, and with a new appreciation for artisanal wares, I began making my own boho-chic clothes and supported local knitters and weavers, as well as a colourful Nova Scotia label called Suttles & Seawinds. The allure of a "Made in Canada" wardrobe took on a wonderful new meaning.

By the time the 1980s rolled around, I was back in Toronto, determined to make my mark in Canadian TV. Because television is such a visual medium, I knew my wardrobe would matter more than it ever had before. And I was overjoyed to discover a burgeoning, eclectic crop of interesting Canadian designers. I made up my mind to strut about in their stuff almost exclusively in an effort to promote the wonderful design talent that our country had to offer. Our shows were in syndication in the U.S., and I figured this could be a valuable platform for our Canadian talent. From Leighton Barrett, Pat McDonagh, Wayne Clarke, Alfred Sung, and Stephan Caras, to Lida Baday, Marie Saint Pierre, Greta Constantine, Zapata, Izzy Camilleri, Smythe, Denis Gagnon, and Paul Hardy, I had a mad love affair with all the brilliant designers who helped dress me, first for *The NewMusic* and then for *Fashion Television*. Labels like Toots, Teenflo, Franco Mirabelli, Joeffer Caoc, and Wesley and Winsa were some of my go-to favourites. And all the while, toiling in those lofty international fashion trenches during FT's twenty-seven-year run, I sported Canadian labels with fierce pride.

I'll never forget the time the late, great Gianni Versace complimented me on the bright orange Sunny Choi suit I was wearing. "Oh, thank you!" I gushed. "It's Canadian you know!" He smiled, looking a tad surprised but also impressed. But I also remember being incredibly disheartened when I interviewed Ralph Lauren in the late nineties for a special I was producing on Canadian fashion. "When I say 'Canadian Style,' what do you think of?" I asked the American design legend. He paused for a brief moment, then shook his head. "Nothing," he responded. I was incredulous at his arrogance at first, but in retrospect, I came to terms with it. Perhaps Canadians simply hadn't ever shouted loud enough on the style front. Or perhaps Americans were just too wrapped up in their own fabulousness to notice much of what went on north of the border.

Even though international fashion borders had started to wane by the time the millennium rolled around, I still worried that perhaps brash American sensibilities had simply drowned out any subtle style statements we were making. Our attention to quality and detail; our penchant for wholesomeness, and sometimes even heritage, when it came to casual clothing and active wear; our classy, slightly more conservative mindset for dressier occasions; and our fabulous outerwear, especially for cold weather climes—these were all points I thought our friends south of the border might have noticed.

Maybe it was just that I was seeing all the contributions Canadians had been making in a very up-close-and-personal way. And I understood the inherent challenges and struggles of building brands in a country like ours. Our marketing budgets could never compete with those of our American counterparts. But still, we could boast a quieter kind of confidence with our wares, and create products we could all be proud of.

These days, Canadian designers continue to make strides, many with their eye on the prize of that lucrative American market. And while I'm impressed with a lot of what I see on the Canadian fashion front, what ultimately still sets us apart from our American neighbours is a kind of honesty, earnestness, and authenticity—that quiet, down-to-earth humility that allows us to see the forest for the trees. We're not caught up in all the hype. We're keen observers and we can hear ourselves think. Maybe that's what's made us such a great nation of storytellers, far beyond what we choose to wear. It's the way we move through the world that matters most. And acts of kindness and generosity, coupled with our love of community, will always be our best accessories.

We Have Already Lived Through This

It is Mother's Day today: Sunday, May 11, 2025. I just got back from the graveyard. Early this morning I drove up to meet my mom and my Aunt Roberta, to join them on their now sixteen-year-old tradition of going up to Grey Mountain Cemetery on this day to say a prayer over their mother's headstone, and to leave her a small pocket stone each, to be added to the ever-growing-and-weaning collection of magic rocks piled up in between my grandmother Florence Amelia Mary Daws's granite marker and the one of the man who she rests skull to skull with. I would have liked for her to be buried with her head facing north, for some reason, not west, but I did not have any hand in these matters.

I brought five stones with me, two to leave for Florence, and two for Patricia, my other grandmother, and one quartz geode already broken into sparkling thirds, a Mother's Day gift for my Aunt Roberta, who raised up two sons and two daughters. I brought my mom some hipster face-tonic-slash-moisturizer and a very nice art card, but I could tell from how she looked at the rock I gave her sister that she would have rather gotten a stone from me, too. We are big fans of special stones in my family. My grandmother Flo always had a small, smooth, sometimes-flattish, round rock stashed somewhere in her purse, or in one of the pockets of her sagging grey cardigan. She called them her worry stones, and she loved them. Would slip one into your palm on a hard or cold or rainy day, or if you were leaving on a trip, or had a math test or a big game coming up. Both stones I brought for my gran were worry stones.

For my grandmother Pat I brought a light grey piece of smooth granite shaped like an arrowhead, because she was as sharp and pointed as one, and another smooth, flat, darker slate grey one for skipping. She loved to walk along the beach with Pearly, her springer spaniel, and skip stones into a calm lake—especially Lake Bennett, which skirts the town of Carcross, about seventy-five kilometres south of Whitehorse. Patricia doesn't have a headstone of her own yet, her ashes have been stashed on my Uncle Rob's guest room closet shelf since May of 2017 because he and his three brothers keep fighting about the proper thing to do with them, so I left Patricia's two stones stacked a little to one side of Flo's headstone, on the concrete pad, with apologies and a promise to call my Uncle Rob and tell him we need to properly lay her to rest somewhere we can visit, and pay our respects, and leave our magic rocks.

My mom and my aunt and I said a prayer standing in a semicircle around Flo's headstone, and finished our coffees, the wind gusting in warm breaths and the little buds on the willows and poplars scenting the air. Then we walked slowly up and down through the tidy rows of headstones, the green shoots of grass showing themselves through last fall's crispy brown leaves. The odd furry crocus still bragging purple.

"I think Dolly Marchewa, our neighbour on Grove Street, is in the next row over from Gran," I said.

"Look, here is Susan Jacobs!" my Aunt Roberta exclaimed, and my mom walked over and joined her to have a look. "Susan Jacobs was our neighbour when we lived in the squatter's cabin in Whiskey Flats," Roberta explained, and my mom nodded, even though she doesn't like to talk about that rented house next to the river much; she likes to pretend they were always in the humble little stucco house on Alexander Street that Florence and Albert finally saved up for and bought, where the seven of them lived in three bedrooms, tucked up right next to the clay cliffs.

"Susan Jacob just loved horses. She read every book about horses the library had, and drew pictures of horses in her journal. She wanted a horse in the worst way, but none of our parents had any money back then, so she would gallop everywhere she went, trotting along on her own two feet, holding up imaginary reins." Roberta laughed and squinted into the sun in my direction.

We walked around for about an hour, locating the simple tasteful headstone for John Frances Leeper, my Grandma Pat's older brother, my Great-Uncle Jack. He was my favourite. I spent way more time with him as a kid than I did both of my grandfathers put together. We built balsa wood airplanes and a telescope together, and he taught me about electronics and how to solder circuit boards and how to operate a ham radio. We could tune into stations all the way in Russia on cold clear nights. We had the same favourite dinner: pork chops with mushroom sauce and rice, and corn on the cob with real butter, and then maple walnut ice cream for dessert.

My dad's best friend Archie Lang is there, too, marked by a big upright headstone, with his widow Karen's name and birthdate already pre-chiseled into the granite next to his, ready for when her time comes to join him. Two rows west of Archie is a huge stone and a carved concrete pad where his parents, Hector and Margaret—my grandmother Patricia's combination best friends and arch enemies—rest together. My cousin Christopher and my uncles David and Kevin are there, too. We visited all of them. Most of my blood relatives who have left this realm rest there, in that cemetery.

I worked here mowing lawns for the city of Whitehorse for three summers in the mid-eighties. It remains to this day one of my favourite straight jobs I have ever had. The quiet. The sun. The smell of grass clippings and wildflowers. The visiting foxes and coyotes. The drive up the mountain every dew-laden morning.

After leaving the cemetery, I drove all the way down the mountain, past the hospital, and across the bridge next to the sternwheeler boat now permanently dry-docked on the riverbank in the park across the street from my condo. I thought about it all. Being back in this place where I grew up. The traditional territories of the Ta'an Kwäch'än Council and the Kwanlin Dün First Nation. If I stand on the corner of my back deck and look across the Yukon River, I can see the roof of the hospital where I was born, 550 metres away from the back door of the apartment I live in right now. If I turn and look twenty-five degrees to the south, I can see the roof of the new, shiny version of F.H. Collins Secondary School. I graduated from the older, danker, asbestos-insulation-filled F.H. nearly four decades ago.

This town is the only place I have ever been from—no matter that I lived in Vancouver for a little over half of my life—and I will hopefully be buried in the same cemetery as most of the rest of my blood and my bones, up at Grey Mountain, just 2.2 kilometres away from this couch I am sitting on while writing these words down right now. I am more than okay with all of this, because I feel it in my heart that I am exactly where I am supposed to be right now. Home. Where my blood and bones rest. I feel connected to this beautiful place, even though I am a settler here. I am a third-generation Yukoner; my maternal grandparents moved here in 1949, and my paternal grandparents in 1952. I think of my friend Teresa who is Kwanlin Dün, and my friend Christine Genier whose mother spoke fluent Southern Tutchone as her first language. Their people have lived here for over 14,000 years. I try to imagine how connected they must feel to this place, with their ancestors belonging to this place for 14,000 years, compared to my seventy-five years of history of bones and blood and sweat on this land. No wonder Christine gets mad sometimes that I get to live this close to her people's river.

I love this town. It is my heart. My home on native land. True patriot love is in me. I am a Yukoner first, since before I was even old enough to understand that I was also something called a Canadian.

Today is Monday. It is May 5, 2025. Seven days have passed since our federal election. May 5 also marks Red

Dress Day, a day to honour Canada's Missing and Murdered Indigenous Women.

I woke up very early, as I always do in the spring in the north, as the days stretch long and the nights wither—and as I often do on this day, I thought first of my friend Shaun LaDue, born and raised in Ross River in the Yukon, the only other transmasculine person from the territory in my genera-tion. We both grew up here, we went to school together, and played floor hockey back when we were both trying and fail-ing to be girls in the 1970s and '80s. Shaun's mom is on the list. I never met her, because she is on the list. I think this is why he ended up in foster care, after she disappeared.

Next, I thought of my cousin Tony, my dad's oldest brother Fred's second daughter. I thought of her husband Brian's sis-ter. She is on the list, too.

Then I thought of Teresa, and Bobbie-Lee, and Sarah from work. Teresa's father, Bobbie-Lee's daughter, Elder Sarah's son, and then just last fall, her son's only daughter, Raven, lost to an overdose. I thought of my friend Tanya, and her search-ing through five generations of matriarchs to find the lost grave of Annie Carpenter, her great-great-great-grandmother. Then I thought of my other friend Tanya. Which always makes me think of Kelly Fraser, lost to suicide. Then I thought of my lifelong buddy Kim, the father of her two sons still living, but mostly lost to the streets some days. I thought of Tyler Bowie. They've never found him. This made me think of my friend Paula. I think they were friends.

Seven days ago, we elected Mark Carney as prime minister of Canada. Not only was his opponent Pierre Poilievre defeated, he was also trounced in his own riding. Prime Minister Carney will be sitting down with President Trump to hopefully unequivocally state (no pun intended) that Canada has zero interest in becoming one. Well, except maybe for parts of Alberta. Except for Danielle Smith, and her merry band of anti-vaxxers and red-hat-wearing separatists holding rallies on cattle farms just outside of Camrose.

As I sip my coffee, I watch a video of Alberta MLA Brooks Arcand-Paul in the Alberta Legislature, verbally trouncing Smith while wearing a beaded rainbow heart. He speaks firmly, clearly, with passion and measured words from his notes.

"I rise today as a proud Nêhiyaw. In a fit of political rage the premier introduced a bill that would make it easier to launch Alberta into a separatist crisis, as if threatening to break up Canada was just another wedge issue. Why now? Why in the middle of rising costs and global instability would this premier choose the path of chaos? Separatism creates uncertainty; it drives away investment; it hurts workers; it hurts the oil and gas sector, just like Trump and his reckless tariffs. But here's what the premier won't say: First Nations must consent to any talk of separation. Full stop. [*Applause.*] Our inherent right and jurisdiction over these lands predates the creation of Alberta. We are signatories to treaties 6, 7, and 8, made with the Crown, not with the province. The treaties are binding. They must be respected. No premier, no matter how loud and reckless, can erase that. The Supreme Court of Canada has already ruled that no province can unilaterally separate, and any path to separation must include meaningful negotiation with First Nations, something this government has no mandate, no plan, and no legitimacy to do. Mr. Speaker, First Nations in Alberta want our treaties honoured, we want our sovereignty respected, and we do not want to become the 51st state. There are many like me—Nêhiyawak, First Nations people, and proud Albertans—who feel the same way. I will take the lead of the late Elijah Harper. I will never, ever vote for separatism because this is and always will be [*gestures with his beaded eagle feather*] INDIAN LAND."

Seven days ago, I was sitting on my couch with my ex-girlfriend eating tacos and watching the election results roll in and tick up and down. I don't believe there was a time that the Conservatives ever pulled into the lead, but in many moments it seemed impossibly close to me. I had to get up the next day and put on my big boy-girl pants and go back to work and make nice with a co-worker who not only voted for, but ran for and lost the leadership bid for Yukon's Conservative party. We talked about the great speech he had made at the Skills Canada awards ceremony the previous week (he quoted Metallica), and when I brought up that Poilievre lost his seat, too, he winced and held up a hand and pleaded that we not talk about the election today because it was all just too painful *for him*.

I admit it. As a trans person, right here, right now, on this day, in this political moment, on this planet and at this juncture, I am having a difficult time forgiving anyone who I know voted for the fascist-adjacent, residential-school-denying, homophobic, trans-hating, anti-abortion dog-whistling, white supremacist party of Canada. I will try to forgive, if I like or love the Conservative-voting person enough, but with this many trans lives at stake, with Indigenous rights up for debate, with a woman's right to sovereignty over her body on the chopping block, with education and healthcare cuts looming large, it will be a long, tall, and painful task. Why again? I wanted to ask him. Was it the carbon tax or because they made you wear a mask? Did you really hate Trudeau that much more than you care about my human rights? The rights of your daughters and sisters? Did the cost of the carbon tax rankle your ire more than the thought of the destruction of this planet?

My Liberal friends are reposting what they seem to think are uplifting memes beckoning us all to now put aside our political differences and be Canadian and get to work saving our country from the mango maniac, and it is hard to argue with that logic, to be sure. But still. Most of my Liberal (not to be confused with those who voted Liberal strategically) friends don't have as much skin in the game as some of the rest of us do.

How do I forgive any of this enough to roll up my sleeves and get to work being a good Canadian?

The first Monday after Trump's second-term inauguration, days after he declared unequivocally—and against all that science knows about the subject—that there are only two genders, and Poilievre scrambled hastily to the microphone less than forty-eight hours later to tell the media he agreed with Trump on the matter of my existence as a trans person, I arrived at work at Yukon University uncharacteristically early. I was having trouble sleeping, and thought I would get a jump on some emails.

My office on campus is located right in between the Samay Thia Harry Allen Elder's Lounge, and the First Nations Initiatives office.

The door to the Elder's Lounge was already open, and Nina Bolton, one of our Elders in Residence, was sitting in her usual spot at the first big table in front of the wall of windows, silhouetted by a halo of pre-dawn late-winter northern light. She waved me into the lounge with one hand and gestured to the empty chair next to her.

"Sit," she said. Not a suggestion. She had her day timer out, and her reading glasses on. "Help yourself to a coffee and a Danish. I have been thinking about you all weekend." Tapping on her phone with her right forefinger.

I did as I was told. The coffee was fresh, and hot. The Danish was not. Someone, probably Nina, had brought in their leftovers from the weekend.

"I wanted to check in with you and see how you are doing. I've been following the news. Watching Trump on the news." She looked over her glasses at me, pursed her lips a little. "This only-two-genders stuff. How are you doing?"

I took a deep breath and then a hot sip of black coffee. "It's not breaking news for me," I told her. "The first time Trump was elected in 2016 he went off on trans people too, on day three. Right after he went after the Muslims, remember? He banned people from something like nine mostly Muslim countries, and three days after that he came straight for trans people. He vowed to erase 'gender ideology' by disappearing us on paper. He said he would take away our right to change our names and gender markers. He said he would erase us. He warned everyone, but no one believed us back then. Well. More people believe us now."

Nina nodded. Closed her day timer and took a long sip of her coffee.

"Years ago I went to a gathering of Indigenous women in Oregon," she told me, her eyes finding mine and holding them. "I met a person there that I connected with right away. We just clicked, like you do with some folks—you just know somehow that you will be lifelong friends. At the end of that conference they told me who they were. That they were about to go on testosterone, and transition to be a male. She was going to change her name and go by 'he.' This person told me that they liked me enough now and trusted me and wanted me to know the truth of who they were. Anyways. I thought of her . . . of him all weekend since Trump went off, and I thought of you, too. I want you to know this: the government of Canada tried to do this with Indigenous people. It was called the Indian Act and it tried to do the very same thing Trump is trying to do to your people right now. Divide you up and tell you who is who and who is what and who is not. Take away your rightful names and what you call yourself. Who your brothers and your sisters are. They did that with us First Nations people. Did you know that before the government recognized the Ta'an Kwäch'än Council, the government just called us the Whitehorse Indian Band? Any Indian living in Whitehorse was registered as Whitehorse Indian Band! Didn't matter if they were Tr'ondëk Hwëch'in or Champagne and Aishihik or Tahltan or Tlingit. It was all the same to them. But our Nations and clans and traditional names mean everything to us. They tried to take our names too, and gave us all the last name of whatever name the white man who registered us had as his first name. That is why we have the Jim family now, and the Joes, and the Charlies and the Sams and the John family, and so on. Our names meant nothing to the government. They tried to disappear who we were in their paperwork. Just like they are trying to do to your people right now.

"But it didn't work, now, did it? You just have to remember who you are, and keep it close to you. Keep your stories and your culture and your traditions and your ways and your knowledge. Keep it and pass it along to your young ones. All of your young ones. They will try to keep you away from your own younger generations, but do not let them. Protect and fight for your younger people, like we had to do for ours, and you will survive this. Just as we did. You might lose many, but not all. They are trying to do their genocide on you, just like they tried to do with us, but it won't work if you remember. If you fight, my girl." She paused. "Excuse me, my Ivan. If you stay proud. We have already lived through this, and you will, too." She hugged me, and I let the tears roll down my face, and hugged her back.

Three days later, each and every single one of my many Indigenous colleagues and friends had reached out to check in with me, to make sure I was okay, to tell me they saw me and were bearing witness to the attacks on my community. Three days went by without a single peep from any of my white cisgender co-workers, about any of it. Finally my colleague Rhonda stopped me in the hallway to give me a hug and told me she was sorry about the state of the world.

Like I said before, some of us have more skin in the game. Some of us have already lived through this, which is why I must step up and speak up and stand up for Indigenous rights in this country we now call Canada. Because to win this fight, to save our collective country and even this planet from the rising hatred and fascism and misogyny gathering on both sides of the colonial border, we need each other more than ever, and this time we all know it. Anyone who is paying attention can see it.

Because we have already lived through this.

I know as a trans person I am supposed to feel depressed right now. We are swimming in fear and hatred and daily escalating attacks on our most basic of human rights and dignities. I have had to cancel three big U.S. storytelling festivals because I am not safe to cross the border, and I do not want to spend a single thin dime in the U.S. until this regime has been tipped and then toppled and trounced. These are without question the most dangerous days for trans and non-binary people that I have ever witnessed in my lifetime.

But this morning, May 12, 2025, I drove up the mountain to the campus, and I walked into the Elder's Lounge, and Jude had the coffee on and was full of ten days of stories for me, and I poured myself a coffee and sat down and knew in my heart that there is no better place to wake up and re-enlist every morning, to do as Woody Guthrie wrote in 1943 in his "New Years Rulin's": *Play and sing good. Help win war—beat fascism. Love everybody. Make up your mind. Wake up and fight.*

ATOM EGOYAN

A Clear and Present Danger

As I write this, I am seated at a desk in Berlin. I'm here to write and direct an original play for the Maxim Gorki Theater. Fifty years ago, I wrote my first plays, for the Greater Victoria Schools Drama Festival on Vancouver Island. This festival, which brought in schools from across the city, doesn't exist anymore. At some point, it ceased to be feasible.

These days, with the massive cuts to German cultural funding, there's talk that theatres like the Gorki may not be feasible in the future either. There's certainly a passion for culture here in Berlin, just like I weirdly felt there was a passion for theatre when I was a teenager in Victoria. It might have been an illusion. Maybe the whole thing was something a few drama teachers concocted so that arty kids like me found an outlet for their crazy dreams.

Culture is based on crazy dreams. In Canada, especially in English Canada, this dream is based on the idea that we have something particular about our experience that makes us wildly different from anywhere else in the world. As The Tragically Hip put it so succinctly, we are always "looking for a place to happen." We make stops along the way, and from those stops come our songs, and books, and films, and TV shows; all of our art.

Some of us find that we need to make a stop in the U.S. We need that huge market to sustain the craziest of those dreams; the ones that cost a lot of money or that can find a much bigger audience. Some of us have been hugely successful in exploiting the U.S. to develop and nurture our talent. But Americans have never been that interested in nurturing us, unless they see dollar signs and the potential to reach their immense internal market.

Like many Canadian artists, I would have never survived in that system at the beginning of my career. My first two feature films were made on grants from arts councils. I don't come from a wealthy family. I was born in Egypt and came to Canada with my parents, who were also born in Egypt, and grandparents who were born in a place that doesn't exist anymore because of the Armenian genocide. Canada was in fact the very first place my family ever had true citizenship. It's very precious to me.

It outrages me when the most powerful person on earth makes fun of my country and belittles its status as a sovereign state. It's become clear that we are experiencing an existential threat to who we are, and we have every right to expect our great artists to rise to this assault against our identity. When I was a teenager, The Guess Who's "American Woman" was like an anthem call. We all felt that coloured lights could hypnotize and that they should sparkle someone else's eyes. But those were very different times and we were living under different illusions. In 2025, there's no way we can take the high ground that we're not fighting a useless war in Vietnam or that we treat our Indigenous peoples better than they do down south.

The extraordinary difference in our makeup from that era so many decades ago is that Canada is now replete with many more people like me. People who saw this country as a beacon of hope and sanity. In the place I was born—Egypt—we had seen the way Canada comported itself during the Suez Crisis. Arguably, we're not even what used to be called a "middle power" anymore, but we're an absolute "super power" when it comes to diversity and internal tolerance. Our system, heavily challenged, has remained impressively "feasible" and is the envy of many others; many of them south of our border.

Will we survive the current strains that are being imposed upon it? Will all the people who have come here from far away "stand on guard for thee"? It's now their home and native land as well, though that's taken on a way more complex meaning. We've felt a lot of true patriot love, but is this just a temporary anthem we're singing together? Will we remain feasible as a united nation given the extraordinary pressures ahead of us? Are we prepared for how difficult things might become? Are we ready to fight battles that might evolve into something nightmarish?

I firmly believe that all of us, perhaps especially us new Canadians, understand what a miracle we're living in. Those of us escaping from oppression and despair didn't realize that we were settling in a country with its own history of genocide, but we are sincerely trying to deal with that. We certainly understand that the U.S. has a dim view of the set of issues we're currently grappling with. They don't have much patience for Native rights and healthcare, but salivate over our natural resources. For many down south, Canada becoming a 51st state would indeed be "a beautiful thing." Never mind that there's nothing remotely beneficial to us about what's being offered. The very real possibility is that we may not have a choice in the matter.

In a recent article in *The Walrus*, Wesley Wark starkly explored the weakness of our current military, stating that we simply don't have the budget for proper deterrence and the advanced delivery systems like missiles, submarines, or bombers to deploy nuclear warheads. Whether or not the current offer to pay over $60 billion to join the "Golden Dome" missile defence system is something we could even afford, the proposed American alternative to simply join the U.S. and pay nothing is lamentable. Bob Rae's assertion that this amounts to a "protection racket" is bold, but it exposes how vulnerable we are. Ever since the cancellation of the Avro Arrow in 1959, we have abrogated an essential part of any national dream: the ability to independently defend ourselves.

The play I'm working on here in Berlin has something to do with the war Armenians faced a few years ago when Azerbaijan attacked an Armenian enclave called Nagorno Karabagh where Armenians had lived for thousands of years and made up the preponderant population. They had fought for that land after the collapse of the Soviet Union and secured the territory after a six-year war. Then, thirty years later, Azerbaijan took the land back in a massive attack that the Armenians—overwhelmed by a much larger and more well-equipped army, and without any assistance from strong military allies—never had a chance of defending. Thousands of Armenian young men lost their lives, and over 100,000 families were displaced from their ancestral homes in an explicit act of ethnic cleansing.

I bring this up because I've been wondering what would happen if this war with the U.S., currently being played out with competing tariffs and sanctions, escalated into something else? What if the U.S. physically attacked our land? President Trump has stated that it is "highly unlikely" that the U.S. would use military force to make the Canada the 51st state. What if this is a lie? While it's easy to convince ourselves that the U.S. won't attack because it would need congressional approval and full military backing, what if the trucks that are transporting food and supplies back and forth over the Peace Bridge were replaced by tanks and portable anti-aircraft missiles? What if troops literally crossed the largest undefended border in the world? Would we suffer the same fate as my fellow Armenians experienced in the territories they lost in Nagorno Karabagh?

There's no doubt that our artists would be writing songs and books and making films and television series after the fact. Well, I'm not sure about the films and television series. They cost a lot of money and take time to make. Who would pay for this cultural response to our loss? Yes, I could write a play, like I'm doing now. A meditation on what it means to lose something that you've been led to believe is yours, something you have been taught is part of your identity and very soul. What role would the rich cultural voice we've sustained for over two hundred years play in this horrifying scenario?

We don't sing songs about the War of 1812. There might be some songs from Quebec about the Battle of the Plains of

Abraham, but my guess is that they won't be quickly translated into English so that our soldiers could sing them while they resist an assault by the most powerful military force the world has ever seen. Armenian young men had a rich tradition of heroic songs and poetry to rally their strength in the war of 2022, but it didn't amount to much except a ton of existential pain and agony. The war was over in forty-four days. My suspicion is that a war with the U.S. would be over way sooner.

I couldn't have even dreamed of writing these words when I was writing plays for the Greater Victoria Schools Drama Festival in my teenage years growing up on Vancouver Island. A few years before, when I was ten years old, I had handwritten a letter to U.S. president Richard Nixon, begging him not to go ahead with a proposed nuclear bomb test off the coast of Amchitka island in Alaska. There had been tests there before, but in 1971 "Project Cannikin," at five megatons, was 250 times more powerful than the bomb on Hiroshima. It was to be detonated almost a mile below Amchitka's surface and the shock would be insanely high on the Richter scale.

A large movement was formed to protest against this bomb, which many feared could set off a tidal wave that would wash over Vancouver Island. My family home, an old beach shack that had no concrete or stone foundation and was made of old wood had no chance. My parents and sister and I would be washed into the seas of Cadboro Bay. I was swept up by the words of this environmental movement (who would later go on to form the group Greenpeace) and put a lot of faith in my gesture. In my handwritten letter to President Nixon, I tried to explain how unfair this was. I said that there was no point to the test, since the world had learned that war was terrible and such destruction was "unimaginable." I licked the back of the envelope with my tongue and scrawled the words "The White House" on the front, and dropped it in my local mail box.

I remember waiting for a reply. I guessed it wouldn't be handwritten like my card. Something in me dreamed of a knock on the door of our rickety beach house. A stern-looking man in a crisp uniform would be there to offer me a letter from the President of the United States of America. Maybe there'd be another man with a snare drum sneaking in a snarling little roll as the letter was ceremoniously handed over, and this little Armenian kid from Egypt would open the official response and nod solemnly as he understood the sheer magnitude of what he had singlehandedly accomplished.

Here in Berlin at this very moment, two of the greatest works the people are absorbing are Robert Lepage's new play at the Schaubühne and Jeremy Shaw's incredible installation at the Hamburger Bahnhof museum. Neither of these artists would have had their careers if it weren't for the support of the Canada Council and other institutions that are committed to supporting our distinct culture. My suspicion is that neither of them (though Jeremy Shaw is also from the West Coast) has ever handwritten a letter to the U.S. president. Are kids writing those cards now? Or maybe sending them by email? Is Donald Trump wracked with pain as he reads these heartfelt pleas from the youth of our beloved land?

My high school drama festival in Victoria has disappeared, and the theatre I'm working at now in Berlin is under incredible pressure. Feasibility has come into question. Right now, as Germany is swinging alarmingly back to the right, cultural institutions are under attack, especially ones that represent diverse voices such as mine. I don't believe that a secret extreme right-wing cabal demolished the Greater Victoria Schools Drama Festival, but I may be Pollyannaish. Would a kid in a Canadian school even write a play about the horrors that would follow if the U.S. attacked Canada with bombs like the one that exploded a mile under the ground at Amchitka in 1971?

Of course, such bombs would never be used, but they might certainly be threatened if our Canadian forces put up a strong enough resistance. Vladimir Putin mentioned a possible nuclear response in Ukraine, though we can only hope that the use would be limited. Canada is way bigger than Ukraine, and a nicely placed bomb in an uninhabited part of the Great North would go a long way to silencing any opposition. Or maybe something detonated just off of the coast of Vancouver Island, bringing to life my worst preteen nightmares of being drowned by a huge tidal wave.

The chilling fact is that nothing is off the table with the person calling the shots in Washington right now. There is a limited sense of empathy and concern for world peace in the jingoistic strains of America First and MAGA. As horrified as a large group of Americans might be about what is happening in their country, they have absolutely no space or energy to fight our battle right now. They are completely focused on what is happening to their schools and universities, their essential government services, the dismantling of their foreign policy and pressures on their precariously free press to spread false information. Right now, we're on our own.

There's something that very few artists like to admit. Most culture doesn't shift the political landscape in an overt way.

Even a huge megahit like *Come From Away*—the musical about what happened when planes bound for New York were diverted to a small airport in Gander, Newfoundland, when the Twin Towers were attacked—didn't seem to have a huge impact on the way people voted in the U.S. Many months ago, at an event in Newfoundland, now prime minister Mark Carney stated to some voters that "we're over the shock of betrayal, but we should never forget the lessons. We have to look out for ourselves and we have to look out for each other, like you did in Gander all those years ago." He wasn't naive enough to state, "I wish our neighbours who we helped would learn important lessons about humanity from the wonderful musical that was such a success on Broadway."

Culture needs to speak to the artists who make it and then emanate outward to whoever is listening and moved by the artist's work. In the extremely tough times we have ahead, I have no doubt that our brilliant Canadian artists will be inspired by this existential moment. Our arts councils will be challenged, but will they always remain feasible? Would invading U.S. troops make a beeline for the headquarters of the Canada Council, and publicly execute the staff caught wild-eyed in their offices and conference rooms? And to rub salt into the wound, would all this happen just as a jury of my peers were about to approve my application for a grant to make my experimental film meditation on the letter I wrote to President Nixon fifty-five years ago?

Art is never a definitive socio-political statement. An article that I recently read here in Germany says that art stands for something that is a mark of human thought and should reflect in its very essence a "tolerance of ambiguity." According to Else Frenkel-Brunswik, this psychological term denotes an individual's ability to "recognize the coexistence of positive and negative features within the same object." Is Canada a massive work of art? We're certainly a huge work in progress. And any artist will tell you that it's heartbreaking to have a work in progress interrupted. The current war with the U.S., now being played out through tariffs and insulting words at the very highest level, is a clear and present danger.

I don't have clear and present answers to these questions. Just as I don't have clear and present answers in the play I'm presenting here in Berlin about the situation in Armenia. In both of these cases, the lands under threat and the cultures they represent and the lives that are living on those lands are precious to me. I won't bother to write a letter to the President of the United States of America at this point in my life. But these questions do keep me up at night. And somewhere in my mind, I can hear the snarling roll of a snare drum as it marches toward my front door.

Maybe it's all just a crazy bad dream. We're all still looking for a place to happen, and we're all terrified of the huge possible stop along the way.

CATHERINE HERNANDEZ

The Things That Need to Be Said

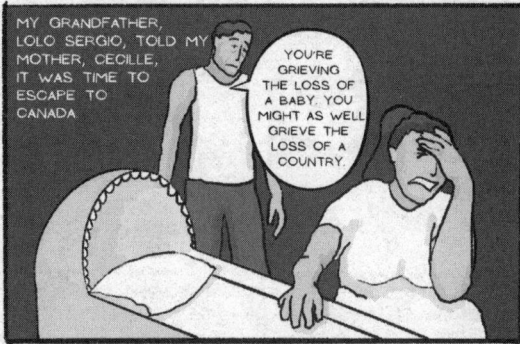

But these days, I've lost the words to describe this moment|

DUE TO MY CHRONIC PAIN & THE STATE OF THE WORLD

~~Happy Birthday!~~
~~You made it!~~

Hang in there for another year?

CRAFTING SIMPLE SENTENCES HAS BEEN A M I N D F U C K .

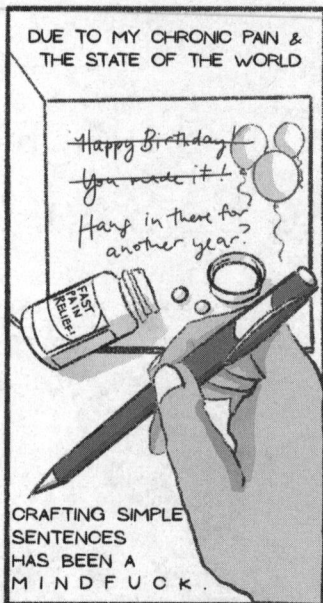

I'VE TURNED TO COMIC ARTS HOPING THE IMAGES CAN SPEAK FOR ME (EVEN THAT SENTENCE TOOK AN HOUR).

FOR PRACTICE, I SKETCH CANADIANS IN THEIR HABITAT.

THE PEN IS MIGHTIER THAN THE FORD

I FILL MY SKETCHBOOK WITH POSTURES, EXPRESSIONS.

IT FASCINATES ME WHAT OUR BODIES CAN COMMIT TO; WHAT OUR BODIES ENJOY.

WHAT SHOWS WE PUT ON,

Increase Profits with AI

(Generated by AI)

WE ACKNOWLEDGE THE ORIGINAL CARETAKERS OF THIS LAND . . .

WOW. BRAD REALLY GETS IT, YA KNOW?

WHAT SEARCHES WE CALL OFF.

WE ACKNOWLEDGE THAT THE FAMILIES ARE HEARTBROKEN. BUT A SUCCESSFUL SEARCH AND RECOVERY IN THIS CIRCUMSTANCE ISN'T FEASIBLE.

DEC 6 2022 FORMER WINNIPEG POLICE CHIEF DANNY SMYTH RE THE SEARCH FOR THE REMAINS OF MURDERED INDIGENOUS WOMEN MORGAN BEATRICE HARRIS & MARCEDES MYRAN IN THE PRAIRIE GREEN LANDFILL

WHEN WE DECIDE TO TAKE A STAND;

AND WHEN WE ARE TOLD TO SIT DOWN.

TO HAVE THEIR ONE CHILD DIE AMIDST
THE ASHES OF DEMOCRACY,

ONLY TO HAVE THEIR LIVING DAUGHTER'S BODY CRUMBLE
UNDER THE WEIGHT OF POLITICAL REPRESSION?

PERHAPS DRAWING THIS IMAGE MAY HELP ME
(MAY HELP YOU TOO?)

THE LAND MY PARENTS SETTLED ON
IS TKARONTO, ON TURTLE ISLAND.
THE ORIGINAL CARETAKERS OF THIS LAND CREATED
THE DISH WITH ONE SPOON TREATY.
WE AGREE TO SHARE THE SAME SPOON,
AND COMMIT TO ONLY TAKING WHAT WE NEED.

THE TREATY ISN'T ABOUT
REPUTATION OR KEEPING THE PEACE
JUST TO BE NICE.

SO LET ME DRAW MYSELF AGAIN, UNSTOPPABLE IN SAYING THE THINGS THAT NEED TO BE SAID, DRAWING THE IMAGES THAT NEED TO BE SEEN, RISKING EVERYTHING, BEING MY PARENTS' GREATEST WISH FOR FREEDOM.

I AM LIVING THE TREATY,
REFUSING TO GIVE UP ON HUMANITY,
REJOICING IN THE ABILITY TO DREAM
OF A BRIGHTER FUTURE.

Letter to My Son

My dear Sandy:

A couple of months ago you asked me whether I thought it had been worthwhile to have spent so much of my time and energy tilting against American windmills. Feeling that there was a certain measure of condescension in the question, I replied with one of my facile, TV-type answers: to wit, that there can be no other real choice open to a Canadian except to resist the Yanks and all their works so that we, as a people and a nation, may escape being ingested into the Eagle's gut, never to emerge again except—maybe—as a patch of excrement upon the pages of world history.

That should have disposed of your question—but it didn't, and the damned thing has been festering within me ever since. It has finally forced me, very reluctantly you can believe, to make a new evaluation of the belief which has sustained me through some twenty years of waging verbal warfare against the encroachments of Uncle Sam. Have I indeed been wasting my time? I'm afraid, God help me, that I have. I can no longer convince myself that we have even a snowball's chance in hell of escaping ultimate ravishment at the hands of the Yankee succubus. And what really hurts is the belated recognition on my part that there never *was* much chance; that Canadians have become so fatally infected with a compulsive desire to be screwed, blued, and tattooed as minions of the U.S.A.: that they not only do not wish to be saved—they are willing to fight against salvation with all the ferocity of cornered rats.

So wipe that smug smile off your face. You knew it all along, eh? Well, I should have known it too. God wot, enough people have tried to put me straight. There was Joey Smallwood for one (as smart a promoter as ever hustled a vote), who gave me a fatherly lecture about a year ago. "What the U.S. wants it will get," he told me. "And if we don't give them what they want, they'll take it anyway. And what they want—is most of what we've got."

That was about as clear an expression of *Realpolitik* as one can expect from the political animal, even if it was primarily a rationalization intended to excuse our political masters for having *already* given the Yanks almost everything of any value in this country. Nevertheless, Joey's point was well taken since those who rule us (they do not "govern"—that word implies statesmanship combined with honourable intentions) have, for their own reasons, long since sold us out. Or maybe they just saw the light a long way back and, in keeping with their dubious professional practices, took the line of least resistance. Some of them, that is. Others sold out with deliberate intent. One day I must tell you the full and stirring story of one of the greatest of all such salesmen—C.D. Howe— and of how *he* put us on the block. Of course, Howe's plan was to sell us down the river on the national scale, and we've progressed since then. Now every single province is trying to conduct its own sellout, in direct competition with the Ottawa salesmen, and it wouldn't surprise me much to see the game, which is called "who'll sell out the mostest, the soonest," reach right down to the municipal level before too long. Hell, what am I saying? It is past that point already. Witness the almost frantic rush of businessmen and owners of Canadian resources to sell themselves and their holdings ("*their* holdings"? I mean *ours*, of course) for a quick handful of Yankee bucks.

Joey wasn't the only one to point me in the direction of acute awareness, and I must add, in my own defense, that I wasn't as stupid as you may think. I realized what the politicians, at least, were up to ages ago. My naivety—if such it was—lay in my continuing conviction that the *people* of this land would not forever continue to acquiesce in this piecemeal betrayal of themselves and of their country. I was much influenced by what took place in Cuba and, before that, in Mexico. I *believed* that if such small, relatively powerless serf states could muster the guts to really kick Big Uncle in the backside, the people of Canada might be goaded into an equivalent demonstration of courage. Alas, Canadians are not Mexicans or Cubans, and I realize now that I miscalculated on a horrendous scale in ever thinking that Canadians would risk cutting off rich Uncle's dole by assuming the posture of a Man.

This is a fact that I am going to have to learn to live with. We have become a prostrate people—by our own volition. Actually the only time Canadians even raise themselves on their elbows these days is to *defend* their chosen masters and to attack, with the bitter hostility only known to turncoats, those who dare reproach them for their spineless espousal of slave status. (If this letter to you should ever see publication, the response in the "Letters To The Editor" column will show you what I mean!)

But there is no point in running on about what's past. My concern is for the future, because the future contains the world in which you'll have to live. So I have a few words of wisdom for you. Here speaks the hoary elder, and if I belabour the obvious a bit, bear with me.

Despite poor old Lester Pearson's recent statement in *Maclean's* that "the Americans are the least imperialistic people in history" (honest to God—that's what he said!), the Yanks now control the largest empire the world has ever known. Its citizens have, as Henry R. Luce (founder of Canada's two favourite magazines—*Life* and *Time*) once put it, now risen to the challenge: "to accept wholeheartedly the duty and opportunity as the most powerful and vital nation in the world and in consequence to exert upon the world the full impact of our influence, *for such purposes as we see fit and by such means as we see fit*" (italics mine). In this delightfully frank statement, combined with one by John Foster Dulles—"There are two ways of conquering a foreign nation. One is to gain control of its people by force of arms. The other is to gain control of its economy by financial means"—you have the essential dogma subscribed to by the military-political economic hegemony that runs the U.S.A. Once you understand this dogma you will have no difficulty understanding the true significance of current events in Spain, Korea, Greece, Formosa, the Philippines, Venezuela, Dominica, and *all* the rest of the sixty-odd serf states which are euphemistically referred to as U.S. "client" states. Note with particular attention that most of these U.S. "client" states are run by military, aristocratic, or political juntas of a totalitarian nature—juntas whose prime allegiance is to the hungry Eagle, rather than to their own peoples: juntas, many of which are maintained in power *by* the United States through classic applications of the principles of bribery, blackmail, subversion . . . and armed force.

Or, if you find such a mass of evidence too complex for easy assimilation, take a long look at Vietnam instead. Observe, if you dare, the fantastic and fearful similarities between the way the United States is behaving in that small and benighted country and the way Hitler behaved in *his* heyday.

Having done one or the other—preferably both—I ask you to consider the reality behind the American claims (ably supported by such pillars of righteousness as our own Paul Martin) to being the world's greatest defenders of democracy. Democracy? My God, it is to laugh . . . but bitter laughter it must be since demonstrably the United States is currently engaged in almost every form of domestic and external brutality, aggrandizement, degradation of the individual, and destruction of freedom which, so the U.S.A. maintains with a straight face, are the *singular* hallmarks of the beast called communism.

And what, you say, is this tirade in aid *of*? Well, it is intended to ensure that you harbour no further illusions about living in a democracy or of being protected by one. You, my son, are a helot, born and bred under the aegis of the United States, and you had damned well better come to terms with this inescapable fact. The illusion of democracy is one that you and your generation can *ill* afford to nurture. You must recognize that hard reality which not all the cherry-flavoured words of all the hucksters in the world can adequately conceal—you are a serf, no more than that . . . and Massa lives away down south.

You must rid yourself of this delusion because, as I see things, there is no guarantee that the privileged position presently enjoyed by Canadians as "most-favoured serfs" will last. The day is near when the Yankees will see no further need to pamper us—they'll own us outright. And then we may expect to be subjected to the same forms of direct oppression that have been inflicted on most of the other peoples inhabiting the two American continents. The steady growth of overt totalitarianism within the Master State itself brings ominous intimations that the good, fat days for the people who sold themselves into bondage may even now be drawing to a close. And remember—a man who sells *himself* into slavery does not earn the gratitude of his master: instead he earns a deep contempt. We Canadians have well earned such contempt—and a wise slave knows that a contemptuous master is more to be feared, in the long run, than an angry one.

Which leads me to an aside I think worth making. Not *all* Canadians have sold themselves. As you are well aware; the French-Canadians in Quebec don't share our desire for self-immolation. They are resisting and thereby rousing our particular hatred and resentment. Why so? It is not because we really fear the development of a true federation of two nations (many other countries live with such federations, and live well); it is because *we* are deathly afraid that the intransigence of Quebec will draw the cold and hooded stare of the

Eagle and thereby expose *us*, by implication, to the furies meted out to helots who revolt.

What I am trying to tell you is that nobody can, at this late stage, reverse the tide. Quebec, bravely as she may struggle, *will* fail. And so your own survival now depends on your becoming as selfishly inclined, as amoral as the men who have brought you and this country to its present sorry pass. You must needs become one of them, and you might as well become one of the overseer class, if you can make the grade. I recommend that you enter politics. Although you have not yet displayed the requisite capabilities for duplicity, cowardice, self-serving, and betrayal which pass for morality in high places, you might improve with practice. It is at least certain that a political career is one of the few available that will permit you to enjoy, with any security of tenure, the benefits accrued by renegades and sycophants.

You might conceivably consider entering the business world, as an alternative, but the opportunities it offers are strictly limited. This is the Holy of Holies, and since its true hierarchy is almost exclusively composed of citizens of the Master State (whether they are card-carrying citizens or only *de facto* citizens is of no import), the chances of a helot rising to those secure seats of power are almost nonexistent. But as a politician you would be employed in the services of the Business God, and as a valuable and trusted slave, you would be deserving of good treatment and assured of a safe niche. There is another course you might consider taking. You could follow the example of so many of your compatriots and anticipate events by journeying to Rome, before the Marines come north for you. As a beginning you could voluntarily enlist in the legions of the Eagle and thereby gain the jump on those of your generation who do not yet realize that the day approaches when the Ottawa satraps will join Australia, New Zealand, and other such in sending levies to fight America's wars for her. Since you have no Negro, Indian, Eskimo, or other dubious blood in your veins, you ought to be able to wangle a cushy job far from the sound of battle and from the stench of burning babies. Eventually you could hope to be rewarded with citizenship in the Master State, and although this would require that you reject all you have heretofore been taught to believe is good in man, it would at least provide you with something you never had before—a verifiable nationality.

I have only suggested a few of the possible funk holes, and you will easily think of many more. The point is that you *should* be thinking about them very seriously, and right now. Time is running out for your fellow slaves who, complacent and myopic as they are, believe they **have** made a splendid bargain with a kindly master. The cold and brutal hour when they learn the truth, and when they learn the price of their betrayal of themselves and of their land, lies close at hand. God help them then, for no one else will wish to, if they could.

The Promises We Keep

1982: East Vancouver

It has been raining all day, the kind of summer rain that is an insult to everyone but especially six-year-old me, who only has three more weeks of school vacation left and here I am, stuck inside instead of riding my purple banana-seat bicycle like the wind down the alley. In the living room of our Vancouver Special, I am sitting cross-legged on the orange carpet, staring through the sheer curtains at the grey sky and greyer clouds. The trees are sodden.

To the south, I see a figure with an umbrella walking toward our house, a person who moves slowly but with perfect posture, a man in an overcoat, holding a big yellow envelope. As he comes closer I can see his fedora, and the cuffs of his suit pants as he steps around puddles. It's Yeh Yeh, and I sigh. It could be someone interesting but instead it's my grand-father, coming home from his daily bus trip to Chinatown. I don't really know what he does there, only that sometimes he comes home with apple tarts from the Hong Kong Café or cocktail buns from the Keefer Bakery. But today, he is only holding an envelope, no doubt filled with boring documents from the Lee's Benevolent Association, the kind he pores over in the evenings as he listens to the news on the radio. Same old, same old.

By the time my grandfather has shaken off his umbrella, hung up his coat, and retreated to his bedroom, I have already turned on the television.

When I was a child, we lived with my grandfather, and his past was almost totally unknown to my sisters and me. We only knew that he came to Canada alone, that he had lived for many years without his wife and children, running his three-seat barbershop in Vancouver's Chinatown, and that my teenaged father had joined him in 1951. We were familiar with his present self: tall and thin, one shoulder slightly lower than the other, a habit of eating bacon and eggs every day for lunch. He didn't offer any stories and we never asked him any questions.

As an adult now, with a child of my own who is endlessly curious about my family's past, it seems odd that my sisters and I didn't wonder about his old life, about the decades he spent living in a single-room occupancy hotel, saving money that he sent home to a small village in China. These were tumultuous political years, not unlike the moment we're in right now, when anti-Asian racists routinely vandalized businesses in Chinatown and harassed the people who lived and worked there. These were the years of the Head Tax, the Chinese Exclusion Act, and then the Second World War, which saw many Chinese-Canadian soldiers fighting for the Allied forces, only to return home to a country where they were stateless and still being denied the right to vote. I was a child of the 1980s who attended public school and the University of British Columbia (which, back then, was sometimes derisively called the University of a Billion Chinese), and it wasn't until I was nineteen and roaming the public library that I stumbled across the seminal book *Saltwater City: An Illustrated History of the Chinese in Vancouver* by Paul Yee, and learned about any of these pivotal events, all of which my grandfather had not just witnessed but lived through. But by then, my grandfather had been dead for five years.

Perhaps we never asked because the history we were taught of the early twentieth century barely included Chinese Canadians at all. It was the building of the railways, blank space, the gold rush, more blank space, so much smooth and boring blank space that our curiosity never took hold. We never asked because we were told there was nothing to ask about.

The blank space where knowledge should be felt personal. Because it *was* personal.

1997: The University of British Columbia

In this class of twenty-four students, an advanced seminar in Canadian Studies, I am the only racialized person and I barely speak. My professor, who I actually really like, is a big man in even bigger plaid shirts, who provides us with a reading list that is typical of the CanLit canon, with authors from long ago paired with more contemporary ones, as a kind of mirroring-through-time exercise: Robertson Davies and Timothy Findley, E.J. Pratt and Robin Blaser, Susanna Moodie and, of course, Margaret Atwood. Including the authors, I am still the only racialized person in this class.

In the middle of term, I finally find the strength to ask the question that has been bothering me for weeks. "Why are there no authors of colour on this reading list?"

Instead of answering the specific question—why couldn't the reading list be expanded for this particular course—the professor launches into a mini-lecture about immigrant communities and their lack of engagement in the arts (he does not address Indigenous peoples at all, which does not surprise me). "The first generation who arrives here," he says, broadly smiling at me in that benevolent way in which many white men with power will smile at me for the rest of my life, "are too concerned with survival, with making sure they have enough money to eat and find housing. The second are too worried about moving up in the world, becoming doctors and lawyers for both the money and the status. It's not until the third generation that we begin to see any cultural output—the books and the films. Most of you haven't been here long enough." And he continued smiling, expectantly, as if I was supposed to agree with him. I said nothing.

What I could have said: my great-grandfather came to Canada in the 1880s, chasing the gold rush. He returned to China after being chased off stakes by white men, after years of working in a laundry, disappointed and resentful. Later, my grandfather came to finish his father's story and stayed, but he also couldn't bring his wife and children to join him for forty years because of the Exclusion Act. My mother came to marry my father in an arranged marriage because all those old immigration barriers had ensured that every Canadian Chinatown was full of men and precious few women.

Yes, my sisters and I were the first to be born here. But my family has been here a very, very long time. None of my family's stories fit this professor's theory, but there was no way of explaining that to him in front of a class full of other students, all white, so instead I wrote my final paper on Margaret Atwood and got an A+.

The history of Canada is marked by ugly truths: the purposeful genocide of Indigenous peoples, the shameful rejection and deaths of the Indian passengers on the *Komagata Maru*, the internment of Japanese Canadians, and many more. None of these were taught to my sisters and me with honesty, or through the voices of the oppressed and abused. Mostly, they weren't taught to us at all. Rather, we were taught to celebrate our multiculturalism and ostensible peace, without any interrogation of what obscured atrocities those things had been built on, or whether the contented diversity we were trained to see was real at all.

As I started to dig into my grandfather's life and the shared history of hundreds of thousands of Chinese Canadians, I began to learn all the components of his life that he had never tried to tell us, and that we had never asked him about. He had gotten married and conceived all four of his children on brief visits home every few years. He renamed his barbershop after my father's birth, calling it Mon Sun Barber Shop, loosely translated as My New Son's Barber Shop. He was one of the first Chinese men to apply for and be granted Canadian citizenship, in 1948. He volunteered at the Lee's Benevolent Association for most of his life, helping newcomers with job applications, housing, and language. He bought his first home, a narrow yellow house that still stands, just down the street from Kingsgate Mall, for my grandmother, when her immigration application was finally approved in 1956.

Do you see the life emerging here, peeking through the crevices that oppression and hardship can sometimes overlook?

Why didn't he tell us any of this? I think the answer is simple but complicated. My grandfather came to a place the Chinese called Gold Mountain and discovered that the promise of it—prosperity, peace, home—was false, just as his own father had a generation before. He wanted to be a scholar, maybe even an academic, but he wound up cutting hair and translating the stories in the newspapers for his customers. He hoped to see wealth in his lifetime, but in his old age he realized that the wealth he had worked for would not be earned by him or his children or, even, most of his grandchildren. He endeavoured to build a legacy for his family that was safe and secure, only to watch silently as his teenaged granddaughter came home from the bus stop covered in mud after young white men pelted her with handfuls of wet dirt while calling out racist insults.

How do you say these things to young girls who are singing along to *Grease* and trying to feather each other's hair? How do you tell them that you wish you could have done better for them, that life is long and hard and you don't even know if the success they want—whatever it is—will even be available to them? How do you warn them that a country that you think is home can betray you, over and over again?

You don't. You see? Simple but not.

In 2020, when the COVID-19 pandemic was sweeping around the world, a woman standing on her apartment balcony yelled a racial slur at me as I walked by with my arms full of dog food. Online, I was harassed for weeks because of one joke tweet I wrote about white people's assumptions of Chinese wet markets. On the television, I saw elders being pushed and punched in Chinatown for no reason at all. Or, perhaps more precisely, for just existing.

Gold Mountain was a promise that Canada never intended to keep.

2023: Toronto

I am sitting at the bar of a very nice restaurant with a dear friend after the launch of my first memoir, celebrating with a prawn cocktail and glasses of wine. When he leaves to go to the washroom, I check my phone, looking for the *Globe and Mail* review. There it is, and it's glowing. But more than that, they have printed photos from my past: one when I was almost nineteen years old and on a trip with friends to Hawaii, and another taken in my family's wood-panelled basement when I was five, my hair in crooked braids. I sent the photos when they asked weeks ago, but never expected to see them accompanying the article at all. It seems so improbable that my old self—that girl from East Van whose best friend liked to date gangsters, who poured rum into the Slurpees she bought from the local 7-Eleven, who learned to play pool in a hall off Hastings Street so that the boys in the Metallica T-shirts would think she was all right—would be invited into the national newspaper of record. I have become someone else in all the years since then, a respectable and reliable author who dresses appropriately and doesn't make a face when drinking red wine, and my current self, the one who writes books and makes slightly naughty but still tasteful jokes at writers' festivals, is the one who has a relationship with the *Globe and Mail*. Not Teenaged Jen who drank piña coladas until she puked. And certainly not Little Jenny with the braids and the collection of headless Barbies under her second-hand bed.

When my friend comes back to the bar, I am crying into my napkin. "Is it the *Globe* review," he asks, concern etched into his face. "Is it that bad?"

"No," I say, "it's wonderful."

"Then why are you crying?"

"I wish I knew."

But the truth is I do know, but I don't know how to say that there is nothing more my five-year-old self would have liked than to be featured in a big-time newspaper, and that this moment is for her, the one whose grandfather lived his whole life for her to have this opportunity. Here I am, being celebrated for writing a memoir, *my* story, and he never got the chance to tell anyone his. I feel pride and surprise and grief. And shame. We can't forget the shame.

So, what are we fighting for now? Am I fighting for the idea of Gold Mountain, the idealized version of Canada that prompted my grandfather to leave his village at the age of seventeen? Am I fighting for Canada as I know it to be, scarred by colonialism and oppression, the deaths of children at residential schools, indentured Chinese labourers on the railway, and drug users felled by a poisoned supply? Or am I fighting for the Canada I think we could be, the Canada that might emerge from this mess of trade policy and misinformation and anti-trans and misogynistic ideology? Or is it worth fighting for at all, when this is the country that gave my grandfather hope and took it away, that gave my mother a home and five daughters to care for her, but that also kept her at the fringes through language and culture? Is it too poisoned from the roots up?

My grandfather chose to stay here. In the almost forty years he lived in Vancouver alone, he didn't once choose to permanently go home to his village, to finally live with his wife and children, to pump water every morning from the communal well, to walk his three daughters and one son to the same school he once attended. He was lonely. He ate almost every meal in a diner. He saved every paper napkin and packet of ketchup. Instead of moving back, he chose to focus on bringing everyone together in Canada, even if it took forty years, one world war, and three immigration policy changes. And he succeeded. My father, my aunties, my grandmother, cousins, and second cousins. By the 1970s, they had all arrived, and my grandfather had everyone he had ever loved, right in front of him.

This, to me, is the most beautiful part of my grandfather's life that remained hidden for so long. Every day he spent alone in Vancouver meant he was one day closer to his family joining him. Every dollar he saved meant he was one dollar closer to buying my grandmother that house near Kingsgate Mall. Every letter he wrote back home was a promise that he fully intended to keep.

I am choosing, then, to believe that Canada can be the country my grandfather once dreamed of, but that it can also be the Canada that I would wish for my children and grand-children. Because if there is anything I have learned from researching my grandfather's life all these years, it's that short-term success can be a distraction and that our long-term goals—the wishes that are core to the very definition of our being—are the ones worth pursuing. My grandfather came here and eventually brought everyone with him so that I, his youngest grandchild, could have every option available to me, so that I could be whatever I wanted. He came here and didn't achieve wealth. He came here, worked, loved, and died, and I became a writer.

And so I choose the same. Like my grandfather, I am choosing to fight for my as-yet-unborn grandchildren's options, so that they can do or be whatever their hearts desire, however they want. In the face of a rising ideology to the south that seeks to restrict choices, that seeks to impose rigidity and acquiescence, I am choosing to believe in the Canada that *can* be—in the Canada that might still inspire or motivate or comfort, that learns from its big and small mis-takes, that honours every death at its hands or in its name.

My grandfather stayed here and fought for us, as an act of love. I choose the same.

No Romance of Self-Assertion

While every attempted American military conquest of Canada has failed, the American cultural conquest of Canada has been far more successful. Because we did it to ourselves. English Canada has been underserved by its exhibitors of scripted cinema and television, and this has helped to foment the conditions for a revival of the existential threat of annexation by the United States.

We can rightfully continue to take pride in the unscripted or documentary format as a truly Canadian art form, the legacy of John Grierson and his Promethean contribution to world cinema having served as a firewall against the incursion of American culture in a way that our scripted cinema and television have rarely been. The continued predominance of American culture on our screens has led to a century's worth of psychic grooming for annexation. We continue to give priority to American culture at the expense of our own. We continue to view ourselves through foreign eyes. In the Canadian spiritual push and pull between inspiration and pragmatism, this point of view has only ever cheapened our inspiration and made more institutional our pragmatism.

I love Canada. I love it sincerely and with the fullness of my heart. I love it with the informed, conditional love that comes with choosing to forge a lifelong partnership, as well as the primal love that every patriot has ever felt for home. My soul binds me to this country and my consciousness is enriched by it. My mother's family fought for this country and my father's family was protected by it. Even if I believed Canada was worthless, it would still be my home and I would do whatever I could to defend it until I drew my last breath.

Of course, I don't believe Canada is worthless. I truly believe that the average person, regardless of race or sex or gender or class, has a better chance at dignity and happiness in Canada than just about anywhere else in the world. Safety, healthcare, education, happiness—these are not ideals but protected rights enshrined in our laws and patrimony, in a fashion usually reserved for tenets of divine providence. And the world can rightfully draw inspiration from Canada as one of its great conservation lands of reason and tolerance. We lead by example whether we realize it or not. We have given more to the world than we have taken from it. We have a legacy of selflessness and service. We are a heartening, con-templative counterpoint to cynicism and brutish avarice. To paraphrase and repurpose a Hugh MacLennan quote about England, I think the world is better with Canada in it.

But every country has its own sickness—local ideals left unchecked and taken to the extreme. And if one's patriotism is sincere, if one cares about one's neighbour, then one is duty bound to recognize national sickness and do everything

in one's power to remedy it. And, left unchecked, our pragmatism and manners devolve into dehumanization and a
particular kind of servility which stand out as the most
loathsome aspects of the English Canadian character.

Seemingly born of our atavistic colonial inferiority complex, and vulcanized by sixteen decades of good humour
and self-doubt, our sickness flares up in different ways
throughout the life of our body politic. Our yearning cos-
mopolitanism has often prevented us from seeing ourselves
in a Canadian artistic context. Our forebears, in large part,
initially preferred British art and British culture to their
local equivalents, and the space they afforded Canadian creativity was commensurate with their interest in it. Compared
to our Franco counterparts, we have always felt less of an
obligation to find our own voice. We have always wanted to
create on par with what we consume, which is to say we have
always wanted to keep pace with London or New York or
Hollywood. Whether we can or not.

An argument could be made that this same desperation to
be validated by foreign eyes is part of what drove white Canada
to inflict systemic cultural genocide upon Indigenous Canada,
through more than a century of residential schools and a
relentless war against their family unit.

White Canada saw Indigenous culture as a pothole to be
smoothed over, so as to make Canada into Britain. They sought
to "beat the Indian" out of not just the Native peoples of the
country, but out of the country itself. This obsessive need to
be taken seriously by other white countries led to a cultural
deletion on par with the burning of the Library of Alexandria
by Caesar in 48 BCE. Lifetimes of art and knowledge were

destroyed, and we have been paying for this act of self-immolation and its resultant cultural paucity for the length of our national story.

The same almost-institutional commitment to the foreign gaze would hinder English Canada's cinema more than any other art form. We have maintained a mercantile dependence on approval and validation from bigger, wealthier, more powerful foreign countries. We inherited a foreign-facing cultural status quo, which has allowed for a select class of gatekeepers with the exclusive Canadian rights to American content to prosper at the expense of English Canada's ability to see itself reflected in the single most important art form of the twentieth century.

Canadian literature would exorcise this demon from itself and be allowed to mature and acquire layers of culture and creativity, like coats of grease on a cast iron skillet. And, consequently, we have a national literature as diverse and messy and contradictory and beautiful and profound as any on earth. As the only country in the world with a reality show competition centred on literary debate, literacy, the joy of reading, and writing have all become elemental aspects of our national identity. We participate in and digest our literature, absorbing its import and fertilizing our civilization as a result. This same patience and space and participation was eventually afforded to Canadian music and painting. And so an ecosystem of art was allowed to blossom—organic and entropic.

But, unlike their colleagues in literature and music and painting, or Quebec cinema, English Canadian cinema was never truly allowed to compete. All of our triumphs have occurred despite, not because of, the Institution (exhibitors like Cineplex)—regardless of the resources and aid provided by our institutions (government-grant-giving entities). Following the advent of television in Canada, our aspirational gaze shifted from the island across the Atlantic to the behemoth underneath us. And in keeping with the precedent set by our consumption of British culture, American culture was given priority over ours at the movie theatre or on our TVs, an artistic hierarchy that continues to this day. There has also been an American military presence, in some form or another, on Canadian soil since the end of the Second World War. And American border patrol officers have jurisdiction over whole sections of our major airports.

All of it for the same reason: pragmatism. Hollywood makes all the movies, so it's pragmatic to just leave the movies to Hollywood. America is the most powerful military force the world has ever known, so it's pragmatic to be on their good side. Canadians travel to the U.S. more than any other population in the world, so it's pragmatic to move the border into our airports. Crafting a national vocabulary is difficult, so it's pragmatic to just use someone else's. It is pragmatic to see the clearest, straightest, least costly path to your objective. It is pragmatic to participate in something that already exists, rather than build something from scratch. It is pragmatic to be dispassionate and swallow your pride. It is pragmatic to avoid rising above your station. It is pragmatic to be in good standing with someone richer and ten times bigger than you could ever be. It is pragmatic to find a way to be useful to someone who can pay you well.

And then it becomes in your best interest to continue that dynamic for as long as you can. Your voice, your opinion, your will to create may flare up, but your pragmatism will more often than not win out against your inspiration.

Because you're Canadian, and Canada's is a story of inspiration forever burdened by pragmatism. Humility—earnest or performative—is as cardinal a virtue as we have, and ambition or the desire to rise above one's station as immoral a vice as we can conceive. We progressed, in moderation, from a colony toward dominion-hood and, ultimately, nationhood, all while maintaining close ties to a monarch an ocean away. We have no romance of self-assertion. Ours is a tradition of evolution as opposed to revolution. If anything, Canadian evolution is a direct response to American revolution.

English Canadian cinema has been on the back foot since the advent of the moving picture in the 1890s. When Britain and France and Germany and the United States started making movies, they, of course, needed people to make them. But this was a brand-new art form, so there were no well-established institutions or communities from which to hire people. And so the cinema of those countries relied on their respective local theatre scenes for writers, directors, actors, production designers, and so on. But when the motion picture camera made its way to Canada, there was almost no local theatre scene to speak of—as most Canadians who found success in that field had to move to Britain or America to do so. For decades English Canada couldn't make movies for ourselves, let alone about ourselves. This was not down to a lack of ability or talent but, as is often the case throughout the long war of attrition between inspiration and pragmatism, due in no small part to a small class of local capitalists with the Canadian rights to something American. And so, by the time there was both a will and an appetite for a truly Canadian cinema, it was fast approaching "too late."

During the Great War, a surge in anti-American sentiment swept across Canada, spurred on and fostered by America's continued neutrality and refusal to join a war which had nothing to do with them. Canadian soldiers carried this antipathy with them to Europe, and if they were lucky enough to make it home, brought it right back. For the better part of the decade following the armistice, Canada swelled with patriotic fervour and pride in victory. The country was also taken by a new sense of national identity. As Bruce Hutchison wrote, "Canada entered World War I as a colony and came out a nation."

And as the majority of Canadian cinemas were in the business of playing American content, the provincial film boards made censorship recommendations inspired by their British counterparts. Fearing the growing presence of American culture throughout Canadian society, and still bitter about America's late entry into the Great War, film boards across the country mandated that images of the American flag were to be cut from motion pictures screened for the Canadian public. This was viewed as something of a moral issue, the recommendation coming alongside others suggesting different ways to mitigate the vulgarity and excess depicted in Hollywood movies.

A decade and a half of jingoism and growing Canadian nationalism resulted in an increased public appetite for a truly local cinema, as well as a belief in its financial viability. As a result, a handful of patriotic Canadian industrialists took it upon themselves to bankroll such an endeavour. *Carry On, Sergeant!* was intended to be an answer to the American and British epic films about the First World War, complete with all the scope and production value of large-scale foreign productions. And, in a highly uncommon example of non-interference, the producers and financiers behind the project knew what they didn't know and believed the best course of action would be to afford their filmmaker an effective carte blanche—save for the sole requirement of being a film about Canadian soldiers fighting the Great War.

And so, the producers offered the gig to British cartoonist and veteran Bruce Bairnsfather, despite his having never directed a minute of theatre or film. With a production budget estimated at a whopping CA$500,000 in 1927, which would have made it one of the most expensive films being produced in the world at the time, Bairnsfather was given an unprecedented amount of creative freedom and resources. All this despite never having shown a single producer, crew member, or actor a script of any kind. And so Trenton, Ontario, and its surrounding countryside were turned into the battlefields of Arras and Ypres, and the local population found work on the crew or as extras playing combatants on either side of the war.

The result is a highly uneven work that functions less as a movie and more as a collection of aesthetic ideas and a pastiche of tropes from nineteenth-century British patriotic fiction. *Carry, On Sergeant!* is by no means a good movie, but I wouldn't call it a bad one either. It is the confused but never boring product of an artistic mind given no restraint and every resource imaginable. None of this matters, though, because two months after it premiered, *Carry On, Sergeant!* vanished from Canadian movie theatres and people reading this have likely never heard of it.

The theatrical landscape into which *Carry, On Sergeant!* opened was one already swallowed up by foreign interests, with local theatre owners all vying for the exclusive Canadian rights to content from American studios. And so, after a fourteen-day run in Toronto and then appearing on a few screens in small-town Ontario, *Carry, On Sergeant!* sputtered to an abrupt end as there were no movie theatres willing to play it. A handful of Canadian exhibitors believed it was in their best interest to sell American culture in lieu of Canadian, and that was that. It would be decades before anyone here would dare to try again.

Carry, On Sergeant! may very well have failed had it been given a shot against big American productions. But we will never know. Because it wasn't given a fair shot. Huge portions of the country didn't even know it existed because America was given priority over Canada on our screens.

Canadian commerce told the people of Canada that they weren't interesting enough to make movies about. Where most movie theatres of the world serve as mirrors of the people and culture from which they emerge, Canadian movie theatres have been windows to the mirror of another people and culture altogether. Even if we are sometimes caught in the reflection.

Throughout the first half of the twentieth century, Canada occupied a certain exotic make-believe real estate in the American psyche. The "Northern" or "Northwestern" film genre was a species of western typically set in the Yukon, populated by stock Canadian archetypes and almost exclusively created entirely in America by Americans, most of whom had never seen pictures of Canada, let alone visited it. And so, even when we saw ourselves onscreen, it wasn't actually us.

But we watched those movies and digested their content all the same, because we had no movies of our own to go see. And over time, by osmosis if nothing else, their fabricated version of our identity comingled with our authentic one, in a depressing symbiosis made all the more depressing for the lack of intention on their part. Nobody in Hollywood or New York or Washington, D.C., ever banged their fist on a desk demanding English Canada let itself be defined by American movies. We did this to ourselves. This voluntary surrender of our movie theatres to American cinema and our incidental appearance in it have done little to diminish the self-doubt and internalized pessimism that occur naturally in the Canadian soul.

We can—and rightfully do—take pride in the achievements of Canadian filmmakers working in the United States, but the cumulative result of all of their art work has been the nourishment and advancement of another culture. And, inevitably, any Canadian flavour in their voice is swallowed up by the dominant ones in the melting pot. Though we have been overrepresented in Hollywood film production since the industry's inception, we have only ever been underrepresented onscreen. And, to be clear, this is not America's fault or its burden. Again, we did this to ourselves.

Now consider the ensuing generations of Anglo-Canadian filmmakers who have self-censored and pre-emptively yank-washed their work in the servile hope of sneaking into American consumption. Ignorant of local cinema, they watch movies exclusively from one particular foreign country and, in doing so, convince themselves that their local cinema doesn't actually exist. They can't have a favourite Canadian movie because they haven't seen many of them. And the ones they have seen are typically born of the same aspirational dysfunction as the fimmakers themselves, and therefore come across as a pale imitation of Hollywood. Which only confirms their bias. And so these filmmakers engage with local cinema as a means to an end, contributing to their own culture as a formality on the road to success abroad. And our system incentivizes them. They are rewarded for having American ambitions because our entire system is possessed of them too.

Our pragmatism has led to a comfortable, closed system of culture and commerce in which we export natural resources and import foreign cinema and television ready-made for consumption in our mother tongue. A foreign culture, it is worth noting, that has been increasingly at odds with Canadian values for my entire life. We consume the portions of Americana we desire just as much as we do the bits of it we judge.

Canadians can and should enjoy American culture. Or any other culture for that matter. But, as the food we consume directly informs the health and functions of our bodies, the art we digest has a cumulative effect on our souls—and it behooves us to be conscious of these processes.

Particularly when it comes to American culture. Because we are fixated on America in a way matched only by North Korea. It is the standard against which we measure, compare, and define ourselves. We have universal healthcare in common with the rest of the developed world, but more often than not it is offered up as the best example of how Canada is different than the U.S. It's the same with social programs, or low rates of violent crime. These are used as examples of our difference from America more often than as examples of values shared with the EU, Britain, Australia, Japan, and many others. Canadian identity continues to be informed by America. We watch their news and know their history. We watch their sports and know their geography. We make a flattered tempest in a teapot every time we are fleetingly mentioned in their sitcoms or late-night monologues.

Some of my favourite movies are American. Same with my favourite music. And people. I am also sincerely proud of the work I have done in both Canada and the U.S., and I am keenly aware of how any success I've had in the former is an almost direct result of success in the latter. I have love for a lot of America, but that doesn't change the fact that vital aspects of our culture are suffocated by it.

Consume whatever you like, but let your consumption of Americana be somewhat mitigated or offset by countervailing consumption of Canadiana. Whatever that looks like to you. Because it is there and always has been. At our supper tables and in our backyards and alleyways and harbours and housing blocks, on our prairies and tundras and in our forests and Legions, our stories continue to blossom and radiate our truth. We have as sincere a culture as any place else, regardless of what the owners of our screens tell us.

These gatekeepers and their equivalents throughout the Canadian story continue to perpetuate the status quo, allowing a shallow pool of artists a seemingly infinite amount of opportunities even if said artists live outside of Canada. And yet our culture persists, helped along and supported by our institutions regardless of the Institution. Culture breeds, messy and stochastic, and we all bear the collective benefits of it. It is there whether we support it or not, but its resonance depends on our participation.

Our institutions like the CBC, the National Film Board, Telefilm Canada, the Canada Council for the Arts, and their provincial equivalents are more important than ever. They continue to provide the only defence of English Canadian screens from American hegemony. Because while there are indeed loads of Canadian films serving as little more than delivery systems for knockoff Americana, there are also loads of wonderful Canadian films that don't get the chance to make audiences fall in love with them. Audiences can't fall in love with a movie they don't know exists.

For the duration of its existence, the CBC has been outnumbered by American networks by a ratio of at least three to one. This on top of having to compete with the exponentially higher budgets of even the smallest American shows. Without the existence of our institutions, the resonance of our cinematic inspiration would be neutralized entirely by the pragmatism of our Institution, and I believe there would be no scripted English Canadian cinema or television whatsoever.

And yet sometimes our cinema and television find a way to cut through the cacophony of foreign voices, and Canadian ones resonate across the continental span. Sometimes, with support and true participation on our part as audiences—and despite the little space provided by our gatekeepers—our cinema and television enable Canadian voices to resonate across the world. We know we can do it, because we have done it and continue to. Imagine what we could do with even more robust intervention on the part of the government in the form of increased Canadian content quotas. Imagine what we would have if we gave ourselves s even a little more space.

If you have trouble doing so, you need look no further than Quebec. Like us, they read their books and listen to their music. They probably do it more than we do. But, unlike us, the Québécois watch their movies and television shows as a force of habit. Their cinema and television are the standard, not the exception. Yes, the Québécois are proud, but any sense of civic duty in enjoying their cinema and television is an ancillary benefit for them. They really just like their movies and TV shows. The cinema and television of Quebec are mirrors reflecting the Québécois people and their culture—and have been for the better part of the last century. Consequently, Quebec cinema and television have attained a level of maturation unmatched in English Canada and their artists are constantly poached by Hollywood.

We can also look to the U.K. and Australia as examples of what meaningful participation in our cinema and television can be, lest we lean too heavily on linguistic isolation as the explanation for Quebec's success. Yes, they have both been waging a similar uphill battle against American cultural hegemony on their screens, but their respective populations actively seek and consume and participate in their own cinema and television consistently and not sporadically. The local character of their stories is cherished and fostered and not dulled away so as to be transmuted into Americana. One rarely feels the ghost of British or Aussie culture in American cinema, but the invisible entity of the Canadian experience can be found in Hollywood movies time and time again.

Because, yes, Hollywood is filled with Anglo-Canadians too. As mentioned, English Canada has always been over-represented in the production of American films. There is one major difference, however, between the Two Solitudes when it comes to how they got to Hollywood. The Québécois make careers out of films so good that Hollywood notices and recruits them; while, more often than not, their Anglo-Canadian counterparts moved to Hollywood in search of careers. Like any artists, they bring their memories and experiences with them, only to neutralize them as they translate their creativity to an American context. And so we get American movies with vaporous implications of Canadiana, our neighbourhoods and traditions familiar to us but dimmed and decreased by their presence in the melting pot of Americana. We see Canada but are told it is somewhere else, and then we see somewhere else and are told it is Canada. We have been gaslighting ourselves for as long as we have been going to the movies.

And, of course, those good movies Quebec makes don't get played in English Canada, and so the Two Solitudes stay locked in their cultural and linguistic silos and English Canada has only ever been worse off as a result. An increase of Quebec cinema and television in English Canada can only help Anglo-Canadian cinema and television. Though it is important to note that the best film to ever come out of our country was made entirely outside of the Two Solitudes and their respective systems.

Atanarjuat: The Fast Runner is the filmic adaptation of an ancient Inuit legend by Inuk filmmaker Zacharias Kunuk, and the first feature film ever to be written and performed entirely in the Inuktitut language. Shot on Betacam in Igloolik, Nunavut, over the course of six months in 1999, *Atanarjuat* made its world premiere at the 2001 Cannes Film Festival and went on to win the Caméra d'Or for the best first feature film. A quarter-century later and the film endures as towering achievement of cinematic exultation that falls prey to exactly none of the pitfalls suffered by the cinema of English Canada since its inception. There is no pre-emptive self-censorship or ghosts of erased localism. *Atanarjuat* is pure, authentic, and original, and we are better for its existing.

I wonder how much stronger our national cinema and television might be if we had a unified industry as opposed to disparate ones, and if French or Indigenous languages and stories got as much space on our screens as America does. Our screens bring America into our homes and now America is led by a raving, incompetent madman backed by an anti-intellectualist death cult 80 million strong. Prone to caprice and issuing rambling dictates like the corrupt despot of a morbidly decadent empire from eras past, this madman has been quite consistent and lucid about his desire to see our country swallowed up by his. And so Canada has returned to its place as a prize in the American imagination. Thousands of Canadians, already struggling from the myriad effects of a global pandemic, are now struggling even more because of American misadventure. And many more will join them. We must do what we can to mitigate this suffering, but we must also not let this suffering be in vain.

We must not mistake this current crisis for anything other than what it actually is—a historic, course-altering opportunity for Canada—and we must not miss the chance to seize on it with everything we have. We must accept that increased unity is not just something to aspire to or debate the merits of, but to embrace fully and accept as an absolute necessity. We must accept that we may need to be somewhat like our monster so we can properly defend ourselves against it.

And if the time of cinema and television should draw to a close, if the most dominant art form of the twenty-first century, or the centuries to come, should be something else entirely, let us embrace it as our own and use it to its full extent to express and understand ourselves with all of our imagination. Let us inspire and sustain one another. Let our inspiration be increased by our pragmatism, not burdened by it. Let us have the security of spirit to give space to ourselves and to evolve our understanding of what that means. Let us embrace our future with the confidence and posture of a people whose capacity for good is matched only by our will to fight.

I love Canada. I believe it should continue. And so long as reason and tolerance persist as virtues in the hearts and minds of free people or people seeking to be free, it will remain nothing less than the hope of the world that Canada continues.

Vive le Canada

And soon we thaw
Voices carry through spring

Not swallowed by cloud
But sharp with the dreams of a country
Too proud to be a nation

My grandad
Through scabbed up Juno
In ancient Normandy

And yet Vimy looms
Unconquerable always

And yet and yet and yet
Brock's corpse but
We, atop the Heights always

We are always marching
A forest, the highway, their sea
Hold fast

And surrender nothing
But give them the universe

And if you want it you are not alone
I am with you all the time

That's Not a One-Off

I had fretted about it for days. I'd read the stories about good, ordinary Canadians getting stopped at the border. Being asked their feelings about Donald Trump. Having their cell phones screened, their laptops likewise. Some even being banned from entering the United States for two years or more. This is what it had come to? A beautiful relationship ruined. What was I going to do?

At first, I decided I'd do nothing. I mean, come on. I'd crossed the border more than a hundred times in my career, and I'd never been met with anything but smiles. Sure, things were tense right now, but banning entry for something on a laptop seemed to me to be a bridge too far.

But then friends and family worked on me. Told me the horror stories were true and provided me with names to verify them. Warning me I could be next. And I flipped. I became almost paranoid, bought a burner phone. Changed my laptop. Deleted social media apps. Cleaned out my carry-on bag that hadn't been cleaned out since I bought it years ago. Just in case there was something in there that I didn't want a U.S. customs officer to see.

And then I got to the border. I was through in less than five seconds. But I wasn't relieved. I was *mad*. Angry at what had happened, and who had made it happen. Trying to trash our sovereignty. Ridiculing our leaders. Throwing thousands out of work. And yes, making me buy a new phone.

When I choose a day to circle, and say, "That's when our friendship really began," I go back 108 years. Sure, there were other signature moments before that, but I like to think December 17, 1917, was the one. Two ships manoeuvred in Halifax harbour, one a munitions ship destined for France to ensure the bloody battlefields of the First World War remained bloody, and that the trench butchery continued, sending millions of the young to their deaths. But that munitions ship would never get to France, instead exploding its cargo in the harbour as the two ships collided and caught fire. Almost two thousand people died, and another nine thousand were injured. The harbour and the city were flattened by what was the most enormous explosion known at that time; in fact, it would remain the largest until Hiroshima in 1945. The sound could be heard as far away as Cape Breton. Half the population of Halifax was left homeless or without adequate shelter.

The devastation meant rescue work was needed; help had to come from outside because, on the inside, so many were dead or injured. So where did it come from? Among the first to arrive in Halifax were those from Boston, in the United States. They had left as soon as word reached them, and they stayed for as long as it took—and it took a long time. That friendship, that bond, has never been forgotten. Every year, the people of Halifax send a giant fir tree to their friends in Boston. It's a tradition that is celebrated when the tree goes up on Boston Common with a spectacular light display draped over it. It's a symbol of true friendship that will never be forgotten, that cuts deep through generations on both sides.

It's also symbolic of everything that's come since on both sides. On battlefields around the world, Canadians have been on the ground, in the air, and at sea, alongside Americans, fighting and dying for the betterment of the world. Within hours of the planes hitting the Twin Towers on 9/11, Canadians were on their way to help, many driving there from across Canada, many arriving that same day. Do I need to explain Gander? Canadians rush to help when natural disasters hit, and Americans do the same for us. Just a few months ago, not long after Trump won the U.S. election, it was Canadian water bombers in the air above Los Angeles, flying through awful conditions to save lives and homes.

Now, sure, we've had our differences, and neither side has been shy about making its views known, even when it comes to being very blunt. On that, we are talking about political differences and leaders who sometimes haven't much liked each other. Think Chrétien and Bush over Iraq. Diefenbaker and Kennedy over the deployment of nuclear weapons. Pearson and Johnson over Vietnam. Trudeau and Nixon over, well, just about anything. "That asshole," said Nixon of Trudeau, which forced the Canadian PM to say, "I've been called worse things by better people." But politicians are one thing, people are another, and it seems we have always found a way to show affection for each other and respect for one another. Until now.

Much of the respect is gone. When Trump belittled our prime minister as a "governor" and us as a "51st state," that went too far. Canadians, even many who disliked Justin Trudeau, drew the line right there. Tariffs only made the division deeper.

This division, this uncertainty, this threat to our very sovereignty, is unlike anything I've ever seen.

Let me be honest. Much of what I have written here, I wrote at the height of Trump's initial wave of "51st state" rhetoric. I was truly upset. I swore I'd never buy American again, never travel on holidays to the U.S. again, never talk to my long-time American friends the same way again. On the latter, some of those friends meekly said they were sorry and said it wasn't them, it was "him." But many others said they didn't know what I was talking about, which only upset me more.

So how do I feel now the initial wave has passed? Has time been the great healer? Not really, but I have mellowed a bit. Maybe politicians standing up for Canada during the election campaign helped; maybe the King crossing the pond and finally, publicly, recognizing Canadian sovereignty helped too. But the issue still upsets me, even though I'm not as angry as I was. I still have no plans for holidays in the States, but I will travel there to give speeches. And I still accept invitations to appear on U.S. broadcasts to comment on Canada–U.S. relations. And I still have friends who live south of the 49th.

The tension that exists between us and our American neighbours may have been toned down a bit, but count me among those who say the relationship will never be the same as it used to be. Most Canadians remain upset. When you change your buying habits, your eating habits, your travel habits, that's not a one-off. That's something that can easily get handed down to the next generation and the one after that.

Think of all the kids hearing the U.S. anthem booed at some of the biggest hockey and basketball games, but also looking up at their parents belting out "O Canada" at the top of their lungs.

Maybe that unity, maybe that swagger, maybe that pride, maybe those elbows up are what we need right now for a lot of things—the True North, Strong and Free. Don't let anyone tell us otherwise.

Elbows Up

I remember when I first heard the phrase "Move fast and break things." I was in the car listening to a CBC radio interview. A self-described "disruptor" was enthusing about how much he and his ilk had already broken. He exuded optimism, as though he were bringing tidings of great joy. I was on my way across town to play hockey in Montreal West at the Concordia University Arena, *Home of the Stingers!*

I play recreationally. And unless I am on the ice with anyone under the age of forty-five, I don't suck. The under-45s grew up playing hockey, and while it is a joy to play with them, it's also frustrating because I didn't start playing until I was forty-six.

I had played no sports up until then. I had watched no sports up until then—with one exception: for much of the sixties, on most Saturday nights, I watched *Hockey Night in Canada*, curled in the crook of my dad's shoulder with a big bowl of popcorn. Howie Meeker, and the Original Six. The names are etched in my cellular memory: ". . . it's Gadsby at the blue line, he passes it to Howe, Howe to Delvecchio and—Jiminy Cricket!—intercepted by Cournoyer, Cournoyer to

Beliveau, Beliveau winding up for the shot, he shoots . . . he sco-o-ores!!!" After 1968, I was too big for the curling-up part and I had already started doing drama classes at the Grand Theatre in Kingston, Ontario.

Organized sports were not part of my family culture. My younger brother played peewee hockey because he was male. He was not consulted; he was carted off in the (pee)wee hours to suburban arenas where my dad diligently tied up his skates and helped him with his equipment.

My dad told me I could grow up to be anything I wanted to be. He suggested I might become an ambassador or an astronaut, or why not both? Neither of these ambitions was outside his expectation of what a woman was capable of, especially a daughter of his. He even supported my ambition to become an "actress," and then, in time, a writer. But recreational hockey player? It was not on the radar. Girls did not play hockey back then—unless they had older brothers and a frozen pond or backyard rink. My own experience consisted of being in net for road hockey games with the older neighbourhood boys. They stuck a stick in my hand and fired shots with a hard ball at my bare shins. Was it worth it? Heck, yeah! But to find actual female ice hockey players, you had to go back to the first decades of the twentieth century, when young women played in long skirts—but they played. Then, like so many other female freedoms and pursuits, hockey was stuffed back in the gender-normative closet, starting in the 1950s.

When I was a kid, the few girls who played on ice played ringette. I first heard of ringette one night when I was ten and my dad thrust me into a game at Kingston Memorial Arena. I forget why. But to this day, I quake at the memory. Those girls were tough! Ringette-tough. Kingston-tough. Back then, ringette was played with no protective equipment—unless you counted the high ponytails and eyeshadow that rendered those girls all the more terrifying. The bladeless stick and hollowed-out puck were supposed to make the game less dangerous. Those girls didn't get the memo. I was speared, elbowed, and mercilessly knocked to the ice.

Perhaps especially in light of my brush with ringette, I am at a loss to explain why I started playing hockey at the age of forty-six. Why not curling? I can say only that hockey came for me. Like a conversion experience. Ineffable. Inevitable.

Ice hockey might be the world's hardest sport to master. But it is also a sport that allows even a rank beginner to feel *AWESOME*. This is a riddle wrapped in a mystery inside an enigma. From my first community hockey skills class at the outdoor rink in Toronto's Christie Pits, I had wings on my skates, my stick was my wand, and the puck—well, the puck was mine. I am a natural forward, happy playing centre because all I have to remember to do is everything. I'm also happy on the wing, where I can lurk netside and pot one, or else pass to someone who's better at potting one than I am. But how does our national sport square with our international reputation as polite peacekeepers? Knives on our feet, sticks in our hands, we chase after a hard projectile, firing it at speeds of up to 108.8 miles per hour, and crash into each other along the way—plus there is no "out of bounds." Compare this to American football: Huddle. Pussyfoot backwards. Throw. All hell breaks loose for a few seconds, then *crunch*. Stop the clock. Huddle . . . And they do all this on level ground with shoes on, throwing an inflated ball that never exceeds a speed of 61.98 miles per hour, and when it or they stray out of bounds—*stop the clock*. So that's one way I see Americans: as a people obsessed with a game in which the severity of injuries is out of proportion with the amount of action; a game with more "show" than "go." A game in which the players' protective padding is fashion-forward.

Then there is the matter of our flags. I remember when the old "ensign" was lowered, and the maple leaf was raised. I was six years old. We stood at attention in the school playground and sang "O Canada." My grade one teacher wept when the old flag, with its Union Jack filling one corner and the Canadian coat of arms off to the side, was folded by the principal with funereal gravitas. But I remember loving our new red and white flag. It's a leaf. It doesn't bear the symbol of an old empire, and nor is it loaded with emblems of chest-thumping victories or grudge-stoking defeats. It's a leaf. I love it.

I hear the American anthem differently now. Not only is it pretty much unsingable by ordinary people, what with its one and a half octaves, it commemorates a battle from the War of 1812. I don't understand why a beautiful, bold, former democracy and would-be "land of the free" would choose an anthem that commemorates a battle from a war they lost—to Canada. Wait . . . I think I've figured it out. A big part of the American "national character" is based on Americans assuming that not only are they the good guys, they are also innocent victims. It is a case of arrested development on a national scale, and we are seeing its manifestation. The current president and his regime claim victimhood as they shred rights and freedoms in their own country, threaten international peace, betray friends, treacherously ally themselves with enemies, and proclaim their intention to annex Canada. And Greenland.

These are a people who jammed Thanksgiving right up against Christmas/Chanukkah holidays. They are a people who may or may not be armed at the Tim Hortons. A people who never got over kicking out the king back in 1776—they've been trying to replace him ever since; witness the cult of celebrity and the extraordinary powers of the presidency, an office which is now occupied by a celebrity dictator. There are a zillion differences between Canada and the U.S. of course, but one that seems salient to me right now is that our parliamentary system of government, while not foolproof, is perhaps a bit more dictator-proof. We are, however, slipping. We celebrate a voter turn-out of 60 per cent. That's not good enough. Our creaky old electoral boundaries mean that 70 per cent of Canadians can wind up being represented by the other 30 per cent. Not fair. Not democratic. We are starting to dig a moat of privilege and access between citizens and our elected representatives, and between our elected representatives and our government. We need more different kinds of people on the bus. I happen to believe we dodged a bullet with the 2025 federal election, but our MPs need to regain the power to speak up for the folks who elected them, not simply kowtow to the party—whichever one it happens to be. We can see where kowtowing gets a democracy just by looking south.

The current U.S. dictatorship did not come out of nowhere. Nothing does. American history is streaked with authoritarianism and fascist flirtations. Charles Lindbergh, for one, batted his eyelashes at Hitler. But let's not forget the

1933 riot at Toronto's Christie Pits—where I took my first hockey skills class—when a swastika-waving crowd busted up a baseball game with shouts of "Heil Hitler!" We like to believe that, whatever our failings as a country, we're not as bad as the States. But at a certain point, moral relativism becomes just plain immoral. Less fascism is still fascism.

If I had to name a favourite hockey player—if my life depended on it—it would be Erin Ambrose. She plays defence. She has all the skills, finesse, smarts, speed, strength, courage, and composure that make a great D. And something more. When I watch her play, I see something I never expected to see in a hockey game. I see her thinking. Hockey-becomes-thought. The effect of this on my brain is strangely pleasurable. Like a neural massage. An MRI might show my brain waves going all Alpha–Theta. Ambrose turns hockey—the rough, non-stop, adrenaline-fuelled sport that I love—into pure thought. I think that is called transcendence. The game itself does not actually slow down, but it seems to do so because Ambrose's perception of it gets bigger—and when I watch her, so does mine. I think the ingredient that makes her play transcend the great hockey qualities that she brings is self-lessness. She sees the whole game. She is curious about the whole game. This selflessness allows her to be completely present. In doing so, she not only distinguishes herself as a great player, she makes her team better, she makes the league better. She makes the sport better. So, while hockey might seem to be the epitome of "move fast and break things," in the hands of a great player, it becomes the opposite. It becomes "move slow and make things." I think that's a pretty good metaphor for a social democracy.

And I think it is significant that we have elected a former goalie as our PM. Goalies are the only players who are on the ice for the entire game. They exhibit extraordinary levels of composure. If you are a goalie, you are always at war—in the sense that long stretches where nothing happens are punctuated by all hell breaking loose. Goalies are calm and on high alert at the same time. They stay in their "house" for the most part, but will pop out of the crease with, at times, alarming derring-do to send a puck to safety, or they will full-on charge out to challenge an attacker. They accept being regularly roughed up with almost beatific equanimity. But if an opposing player gets in their crease—the blue paint that demarcates their "house"—the goalie will spear that player mercilessly with the butt of their stick, or will trip them and send them into the boards. Players protect the goalie with the loyalty and ferocity with which they would protect their moms. "Don't you f***in' touch my goalie!!" Because your mom does the same for you and then some. The puck stops with the goalie.

I think Americans should change their national anthem from "The Star-Spangled Banner" to "America the Beautiful." They'd have to change some lyrics and shorten it, but the melody is beautiful, and some of the words have always brought tears to my eyes: "O beautiful for spacious skies / For amber waves of grain / For purple mountain majesties / Above the fruited plain. America! America! God shed His grace on thee / And crown thy good with brotherhood / From sea to shining sea."

My only gripe with "America the Beautiful" is that I never refer to the United States as America. This is because America is a continent. Two continents. In a triumph of classic American branding, the U.S. co-opted the name *America* for itself. I would, however, overlook this in their anthem if they were to change it.

Bring on America the Beautiful. Bring on the opposite of the Ugly American—this was the title of an American novel published the year I was born, and it became a catchphrase. Throughout my childhood, the U.S. was in flames of unrest born of racism, and protest against the Vietnam War. I remember when the students at Kent State were shot dead by the National Guard. I was afraid to grow up and go to university.

But. I am a little bit American, because I am wholly Canadian. We are interlinked. I've always believed Canadians should have a one-third vote in American presidential elections. And that the rest of the world should have a sliding-scale percentage of a vote. I am grieving what is happening in the U.S.

Dear America (I know you prefer that name),
Thank you for the fun and the excitement and the art and the pop culture and the boldness and the many *yes*es that you say, especially when Canada so often says *well let's not rush into this*. Thank you for rushing in with crazy creativity, bold ideas, and risky investments, and thank you for the maddeningly precious, sometimes just dumb, but usually amazing former NEA. Thank you for a being a place where Canadian artists and entertainers who hit glass ceilings and brick walls at home have been able to soar—and, yes, finally find work in Canada after having made it in the States.

Thank you for my children, both of whom were born in the U.S. Thank you to their birth mother, an

American woman who, like so many Americans, had to chart her path without the supports Canadians take for granted—"basics" like healthcare, good public education, and social assistance. She is a brave, strong, brilliant, and independent woman who made the conscious decision to place her babies in a Canadian family.

To the few among my American cousins who voted for Trump: I remember that the letters you wrote when we were kids were not quite literate, and I guess it stands to reason that, as products of a tattered school system, you voted for someone who has opted to simply toss the whole thing into the garbage. But yes, I'm mad at you.

To my American friends and colleagues: we will always be friends, and it's more important than ever that we remain colleagues.

Thank you to all the Americans who are protesting every day. Thank you to all of you who are still talking and listening to one another. Thank you to all of you who are striving to find a peaceful way through.

My favourite hockey players now are women. But back in the days when I was curled up in the crook of my dad's shoulder, my favourite player was Gordie Howe. Howe was a great player. And in the way of greatness, he was consistent. He was a forward who played a strong two-way game, and he wanted the puck. He did not look for a fight, but if you went into the corners with him, beware. Gordie Howe's elbows were up. And they were lethal. If you encountered those bony boomerangs, you might not finish out the game. I feel the elbow is a peculiarly Canadian metaphor: an elbow is a weapon, and it is also the seat of the "funny bone." Not for nothing is American comedy one of Canada's most successful exports. And not for nothing is pro hockey disproportionately peopled with Canadian players.

So, from the days when I watched *Hockey Night in Canada* with my dad, whenever I hit a snag at school—or, later, as I embarked on my career in the physically moderate but psychologically extreme field of acting—he would say, "Keep your elbows up in the corners." My dad died in 2017. He lived long enough to see his prediction of the demise of American democracy begin to surface like a U-boat in the St. Lawrence. But he died before he could see his advice to me become a national saying in the face of American threats to Canada's existence.

It is still common to hear these threats ascribed to Donald Trump by name. He is still the butt of endless jokes; his wild proclamations and absurd behaviour are a bottomless source of laughs. But I no longer laugh at Trump. And when I discuss the threats to our country, its people, and all its inhabitants, to the water, the land, the sky—to Canada the Beautiful—I no longer temper those threats by ascribing them to Trump. He speaks for his regime, both elected and unelected. And he speaks for the American people. They elected him. The American people wish to deprive us of our sovereignty. The American people wish to seize and plunder the land and its creatures, including its people, its water and its sky. The American people wish to do this to an extent undreamt of by our worst Canadian offenders—those among us who see Canada the Beautiful as a collection of monetizable resources.

The United States of America has stated its intention to take over our country, to end our democracy, and to steal our resources. When the American people decide that they do not wish to do this, we will know, because the current dictatorship will have been deposed. I hope that will happen via an election. For now, my funny bone is numb. But my elbows are sharp.

An Indian at the White House

On March 24, 2016, I went to the White House. Well, sort of. Technically, it was the Eisenhower Executive Office, but it's within the larger complex at the heart of Washington, D.C., and the American Empire. The security certainly suggested that we were close enough to warrant the many gates and bulletproof glass panes to pass through to gain entry. So, that's good enough for me.

I was there for a film screening, naturally, as that was my business at the time. I was working at the Toronto International Film Festival as the head of its cinema and gallery programming team, and I was already well established within the Indigenous film sector. And that's how I got an invite to this particular event. TIFF had considered it enough of an honour to cover my travel expenses. The invite came from Chris Eyre—director of *Smoke Signals*, most famously. A film he had produced, called *The Seventh Fire*, was to be shown and followed by a panel discussion. I have found the panel discussion on YouTube, though can't find myself in the audience—but believe me, I was there.

The film is a rather raw documentary about a First Nations gangster seeking redemption through embracing his Anishinaabe culture. It's named after a prophecy that our people have about a time when we will reignite our culture, its teachings and way of life, so that we may survive. It's a prophecy that predicts the end of colonialism, when the earth has been almost destroyed, and prescribes the way to survive.

The film is gripping and emotional, although not necessarily my type of movie, but I wanted to attend to show my support for those involved, and because when the hell else was I going to get an invite to the White House/Eisenhower Executive Office? Never, that's when. So I went.

I was late, as I underestimated evening traffic in D.C., however I did get to see the reception area, which is called the Treaty Room. Now, there are two Treaty Rooms—one in the actual White House, which is apparently used as a den by the president, and one in the Eisenhower building. I was in the second one. It's used for exactly these sorts of events, or at least it was before the darkness came. One can only imagine now.

If you've ever been inside a colonial capital building—not surprisingly, it doesn't matter which colonial power—then you can probably guess the vibes of the Treaty Room at the White House. It is an ornate room inside a castle, so it has a grotesque beauty that tends to send shivers up this Nish's spine, even though I know the food will probably be good.

The irony of hosting a screening of this film with a bunch of Indians in the audience, and having us visit the Treaty Room of a nation notorious for breaking treaties with First

Nations, was, of course, not lost on anybody. But we were still all there, because that's what we do. As we try to gain footholds, it requires us to be present in spaces just like this one. Nearly a decade later, as I write this, I've now spent much time in rooms not so different from that one, with other governments known for their treaty-breaking ways.

After the screening I went out to a swanky restaurant with the cast, the director, and Chris. It was a loud place that overlooked the White House and surrounding landmarks. It was quite lovely, even as I worried about getting back to my more suburban hotel.

This event occurred during Barack Obama's second term, and just a year before Canada would celebrate its sesquicentennial. Justin Trudeau had only been elected the year previous, and he was still riding high on the wings of his Haida tattoo. The Truth and Reconciliation Commission had published its findings and ninety-four calls to action a year earlier. In other words, if there was ever going to be a gathering of Indians to watch a movie at the White House, this was exactly the time. It's certainly hard to imagine it happening again.

Canadians now find themselves in a position familiar to First Nations on Turtle Island, holding one end of a treaty while the other end is shredded. Between 1778 and 1871, the United States government entered into more than 500 treaties with First Nations. Of those, 374 were ratified by Congress. In 1871, Congress decided that these nations were no longer nations, and the treaty-making era ceased. Of the 374 treaties ratified, guessing that zero have been honoured would be an extremely safe bet. Many of these treaties were coerced at gunpoint, and the U.S. just didn't imagine honouring many more.

Canada has signed more than seventy treaties with First Nations, and they tend to be labelled either historic or modern, with treaties signed before Confederation deemed historic, while the eleven signed after are called modern or the Numbered Treaties. Canada's history with treaties is slightly better than the empire's to the southern side of the Medicine Line. Canada still enters treaties (whether these are good agreements, or coerced, is a story for a different book), and the government and provinces are currently settling long-standing treaty disputes like the one with my community.

Genaabajing is one of twenty-one communities that signed the Huron-Robinson Treaty of 1850. That treaty included a verbal process and a written one, and since the written one was in English, you can guess what happened. The treaty written down was not the one agreed to verbally. And even if it was, Canada—or the Crown—rather quickly stopped honouring the treaty anyway. The communities sued almost twenty years ago, and won. The compensation is in the billions.

It was in the first Trump administration that Canada got a sense that its treaties with the U.S. might be in danger when he cancelled the U.S.–Canada–Mexico free trade agreement. He did the same thing when he was re-elected in 2024, cancelling the treaty his own government had negotiated.

In 1779, the Haudenosaunee gave the nickname Hanödaga:yas to George Washington. It translates to "Town Destroyer" or "Village Eater." It's a term for the nature of the colonizer, those that come in peace but lay waste to all that they touch.

Trump is just the modern incarnation of this historic monster.

But this time, it's the villages and towns of colonialism that are under threat. The new colonizer will seek to kill all the buffalo, whatever form they take today, and stack their skulls in pyramids of destruction. This is their nature.

For a culture that brought this violence—and has manifested its fear of it being returned upon them in decades of sci-fi and horror movies—its turn toward itself is no doubt scary. This contributes to the slow reaction to what is the obvious disintegration of the systems of resistance that we are witnessing.

The fact that Black and brown people have been sounding this alarm for generations does not seem to have mattered. Even though some have always lived with America being an authoritarian state, those that benefitted the most from it have rarely wanted to hear the truth. Perhaps if they had actually got to know any of us, they might have learned the strategies we used to survive the coming of the village eaters the last time. Perhaps it is time for them to embrace the prophecy of the seventh fire themselves, so that it isn't just us that survives this moment.

These strategies are acts of intergenerational resistance. It can require the breaking of laws in the present to preserve justice in the future, especially when those laws seek to reduce the possible futures available. Many of the acts taken are little spoken about because these moves must be made in secrecy, away from the means of surveillance that those who would consume our villages employ. Our resistance will not be borne on the information systems they control; it will sprout from the ways we communicate, and from shared physical spaces where these acts of resistance will spread. Perhaps most importantly, it is to understand deeply that the land is the both the source of our resistance and our salvation. Canadians need to truly reimagine their relationship with the land, and perhaps even consider its centrality to a new national identity born of this moment—not as an arena of dominion, but one of right relations. That it is the treaty we make when we are born from the land.

Treaties with the U.S. are unlikely to serve anyone well in the immediate future. Instead, Canadians should look toward the treaties they already have. There are nations here that know what it is to resist a colonial threat. We are still doing it. This is in fact the differentiation point from the U.S. that would best serve Canada in this moment. We need a move away from the systems that these two colonial siblings share, and it is time for Canada to embrace a different nature. One that, instead of denying its history, as this place has done for so long, faces it. Stares at its own eyes in the reflecting pool, and dives deep to emerge in a new form.

We will still be here, as we always have been, but it's time for these nations to make the changes necessary to live with us—or face the flames that are coming from the fire they started and fed with us as their fuel.

The North American Pattern

As I have little that's fresh to say about the United States and our relationship to it, I'm obliged to reiterate here arguments previously published.

A truism or two first.

Canada has not one, but two cultures. If the French is cocooned by language, the English, we are told again and again, is threatened by American-made vileness. For years Faulkner, *Classic Comics*, Ed Sullivan, *Partisan Review*, Elvis Presley, Henry Miller, and Huckleberry Hound have all been spilling freely over the border, stupefying our young ones; but recently Canada has grown resentful. Canadians, without yet building an Uhuru Stadium, unless Expo qualifies, have become proud to be . . . well, Canadians, and the upshot has been an increasingly truculent, occasionally touching national pursuit of something or other we can be true to. A heritage. A tradition. *Anything*.

What is so embarrassing is that while we are determined to defend our culture against any comer, nobody is sure what our culture is, how it differs from the British or American, or come to think of it, if we even have one. Once we were content with a modest but coy definition. We were neither British nor American, but something else. Something nice, very nice. The continued quest for that "something very nice" has created one of the few original Canadian enterprises, the What-Is-Our-Identity business, and a spiteful subsidiary, anti-Americanism.

Alas, I'm not anti-American. Far from it. As a boy in Montreal I can remember that my family was convinced that we gained from dissension between Canada's two cultures, and we looked neither to England nor to France for guidance. We turned to the United States. The real America.

What America, America meant to us in those days was Roosevelt, the Yeshiva College, Danny Kaye, a Jew in the Supreme Court, the *Jewish Daily Forward*, Max Baer, Mickey Katz records, Dubinsky, Mrs. Nussbaum of Allen's Alley, and Gregory Peck looking so cute in *Gentleman's Agreement*. Why, in the United States a Jew even wrote speeches for the president. Returning cousins swore they had heard a cop speaking Yiddish in Brooklyn. There were the Catskill hotels, Jewish soap operas on the radio, and above all, the earthly pleasure grounds, Florida. Miami! No manufacturer had quite made it in Montreal until he was able to spend a month each winter in Miami.

We were governed by Ottawa, we were also British sub-jects, but our true capital was certainly New York. Success was (and still is) acceptance by the United States. For a fighter this meant a main bout at Madison Square Garden, for a writer or artist, praise from New York critics, and for a businessman, a Miami tan. During the war, in Montreal, our heroes were largely American or American-made. We understood intuitively, for instance, that no Canadian soldier ever would have snarled, "Send us more Japs!" He might have come up with, "No offense to peoples of Asian extraction, but I think we could cope with more Japanese here." Our hearts went out, not to the Black Watch, but to John Wayne and the U.S. Marines. Others precious to us were John Garfield, Joe DiMaggio, and Frank Sinatra, and the most serious crisis of the war was the ban on American comic books, which meant that we were deprived of *Captain Marvel* and *The Batman* for the duration and had to put up with drab Canadian imitations.

It was nice, very nice, that Walter Pigeon, *Canadian-born*, was a Hollywood star, but if you wanted Lauren Bacall you had to be Bogart. An urban American.

By the time we reached university we were, as I recall it, thoroughly embarrassed to be Canadians. Charged with it, we always had a self-deprecating joke ready. Then one or perhaps two of us dared to say out loud, "I'm going to be a writer." The immediate rejoinder was, "What, you're going to be a Canadian writer?" It was a confession of limitation not an honourable ambition.

As recently as 1960, when I returned to Canada after several years abroad, I found that many Canadians were still prepared to blame the Americans for all our failures. If only *they* would leave us alone, we would be big, important, and above all, cultural. We were urged to buy (and read) Canadian magazines, which were being driven into the ground by "unfair" American competition. "If the Canadian magazines are allowed to die," a concerned Hugh MacLennan said, "we would become the northern equivalent of a banana republic." But among those publications seeking shelter under a cultural umbrella, *Chatelaine*, a specialist in recipes and royalty stories, was typical. The sad truth was, and still is, that most educated Canadians would rather pay more for American periodicals than have the best Canadian magazines, because without them we would feel intellectually cut off.

As Morley Callaghan once said, "The effort to direct our culture away from the sources of light is all very well for speeches by ministers of education . . . but it has nothing to do with the real problem . . . Canada is a part of the North American cultural pattern. We have our own idiosyncrasies up here, you know, our own peculiar variation of the culture pattern . . . But it is still definitely American."

Living in London for so long, as I have, the lesson, if it ever had to be learned, is that we Canadians are North American by tradition and culture, and, compared to how foreign we are in England, the difference between, say, a Torontonian and somebody from Denver is no more than a regional nuance.

When I return to Canada from time to time, what I always find most tiresome is the cultural protectionism, the anti-Americanism. No heritage is worth preserving unless it can survive the sun, the mixed marriage, or the foreign periodical. Culture cannot be legislated or budgeted or protected with tariffs. Like potatoes. I also feel it's time we recognized that the best, as well as the worst, influences in the world reach us from the United States, and furthermore, it is most likely that we will always be an American satellite.

However, if I still feel the longest unmanned frontier is an artificial one, I no longer look forward, as I once did, to the day when it might disappear and we would join fully in the American adventure. Vietnam and Ronald Reagan, among other things, have tempered my enthusiasm. Looked at another way, yes, we *are* nicer. And suddenly that's important.

PAUL MYERS

The Canadiafornian

Growing up in Toronto in the 1960s, my early awareness
coincided with Canada's very public exploration and declaration of its national pride. Though the significance of adopting
the maple leaf flag in 1965 was beyond my young comprehen-
sion, its clean, modern, red-and-white simplicity resonated as
something new and exciting. The centennial celebrations of
1967 remain vivid: the Confederation Train's stop in nearby
Don Mills, Ontario, thrilled me, and our family camping trip
through the Laurentians en route to the futuristic pavilions
of Expo 67 in Montreal showcased a modern nation that blew
my young mind. At a vibrant one hundred years old, Canada
felt undeniably cool to a boy like me, and I felt a quiet gratitude for my parents' journey from Liverpool, England, which
had offered us a life in this young and evolving country. Of
course, I was then unaware of our internal dialogues and the
burgeoning national recognition of the distinct contributions
of Québécois and Indigenous voices within our "cultural
mosaic." Yet I instinctively understood that, unlike the
American "melting pot," Canada seemed to invite Europeans,
Africans, adventurers from the British Commonwealth, and

even draft-dodging Americans to contribute their skills and ambitions to defining, populating, and fostering the idea of a great nation.

In time, I also became aware of the enduring national conversation about our identity and aspirations. While a singular definition has always been elusive, a common thread seems to be defining ourselves in contrast to our American neighbours. To ironically echo Kendrick Lamar, given his history with Toronto's Drake, our view of those south of the border is simply, "they not like us."

I come by this knowledge first-hand, because I am a Canadian living in the U.S.A.

While I am Canadian by birth and by nature, my wife and I left Toronto in 1997, captivated by Northern California. Work visas transitioned to green cards, and eventually we bought a perfect little bungalow in Berkeley, across the bay from San Francisco. A tall palm tree stands beside a towering evergreen in our backyard, the latter a constant reminder of home. By 2014 (during the Obama years, I should add), seeking full democratic participation and community engagement, we both became U.S. citizens. For me, the dichotomy of being a dual citizen shapes all questions of Canadian identity—and equally, what it isn't.

I love Canada. I love California. I am the Canadiafornian.

Presently, I hold a U.S. passport but maintain my Canadian one. Adding a layer, I keep a U.K. passport, courtesy of my British parents, and I like to joke that I'm not just *cosmopolitan*, my trio of passports are like three flavours of ice cream, which makes me *Neapolitan*.

Crucially, my world view remains staunchly Canadian, but with a light fleece replacing a seasonal parka. I still cherish the values that Canada bred in me: a belief in fairness, kindness, and what we used to call "multiculturalism." I am an advocate for, and a grateful beneficiary of, a publicly funded healthcare system, which falls under a broader national aspiration toward social justice (and I have a very Canadian readiness to recognize the times in our history when we've fallen short of that promise).

Being Canadian in 2025 has involved the constant and compulsive sharing of memes, TikToks, and Reels dissecting who we are, who we'll never be, and how Canada steadfastly remains a friendly yet fiercely independent sovereign nation. While I've written for U.S. and U.K. publications, I stay closely connected to Canadian media, particularly cherishing my occasional CBC appearances, which always feel like going home, regardless of my actual location.

I stay informed on news from both sides of the border, thanks partly to a daily text exchange with my two brothers, one in Mississauga, the other in New York. We were raised with a healthy skepticism toward jingoistic nationalism and empty flag-waving, but when our core values and identity are challenged, the maple leaf flags proudly emerge.

One positive outcome of the recent "51st state" nonsense has been the renewed focus on our identity. The familiar rallying cry of "elbows up" implies an aggressively defensive stance, as opposed to a jingoistic threat of aggression. As Canadians, we aim to be good neighbours, just as I believe most Americans want to be good neighbours to us.

To be a Canadiafornian is a constant act of translation: miles to kilometres, Canadian to American spellings (*humour* vs. *humor*), and converting my media work fees. (My wife's name is Liza, which is spelled with either a "zed" or a "zee" depending on who I'm talking to.)

We blend in so seamlessly that most Americans might not even realize we're Canadian, walking among them like undercover agents, noting the contradictions of American life while simultaneously explaining "snow days" to Californians. Arguably, this could be the reason that there is typically no greater cheerleader for Canada than a Canadian expat. We're begging you to notice that we're not like you. In our California home, we have a miniature clay Mountie statue in the dining room, I have a Canadian flag poster in my studio, and I rotate through a variety of proudly Canadian T-shirts, some emblazoned with vintage CBC logos, and have a distinct preference for shirts bearing the band name Sloan.

No matter how long we live stateside, we still manage to view the United States through an outsider lens, and I've long believed this perspective affords Canadians certain insights that Americans—raised on American exceptionalism—might have missed. Our comparative humility lets us offer constructive criticism in an unthreatening manner.

And there's plenty to criticize; the Canadian expats I know down here, and quite a few Californians, share my disbelief at the political inaction regarding sensible gun control and the lack of a national healthcare system, which basically means that if you survive getting shot, the threat of medical bankruptcy looms over your hospital stay.

Living in California is a continuous process of adaptation and discovery—navigating a new cultural landscape, embracing a different climate—and while it's nearly impossible to get truly good poutine, I still thrive on the Golden State's energy and the pioneering spirit of immigrants from all over the world who came to this place, just as we did, to reinvent themselves in the Wild West.

But it isn't Canada. Canada is home.

The Sky Is
Falling . . . Again!

I recall a political cartoon that was published in a Canadian paper in the early 2010s. It featured a silvery-, wild-haired man flapping about with an encyclopedia under his arm. Bright yellow chicken feet stuck out from his well-tailored suit. He was yelling, "It's too late to save Canada!"

I was offended on his behalf, but the subject of the cartoon didn't give much of a damn. He said the rag that published the thing was being slowly sold off to the Americans, so what could we expect?[*]

My father, Mel Hurtig, was a lifelong defender of Canadian independence. He believed that too many decisions affecting Canadians were being made outside Canada's borders. In his landmark book *The Betrayal of Canada* (1991), he warned, "We have become a country where too many of our major

---

[*] As of 2025, Postmedia, which runs the great majority of this country's newspapers, is 66 per cent owned by a U.S. investment company.

corporations are no longer Canadian, where too many decisions affecting our lives are made in foreign boardrooms."

He was not alone. Walter Gordon, a former federal finance minister and chair of the 1957 Royal Commission on Canada's Economic Prospects, had come to a similar conclusion decades earlier when he cautioned that if we allowed control of our economy to slip out of Canadian hands, then we would lose the ability to make the political decisions that reflected our own values.

Both men argued that economic sovereignty is the foundation of political freedom. For them, it wasn't enough for Canada to have its own parliament and flag if the key levers of economic power—energy, finance, media, industry—were increasingly controlled by foreign, often American, interests.

Despite decades of warnings, the core issues my dad—and people like Walter Gordon, Maude Barlow, and David Orchard—raised remain unresolved, and in many ways have worsened. Canadian corporations are regularly sold to foreign buyers, with little resistance from government regulators. Much of Canada's natural resource sector is controlled by multinational firms. Media and cultural content are overwhelmingly influenced by American platforms. Mel described this phenomenon as a slow-motion surrender, warning that one day we'd all wake up to discover there was very little left to call our own.

Economic sovereignty is not about isolationism. It is about having the power to make decisions in the national interest, based on Canadian values and priorities. Gordon understood this deeply, and he emphasized the importance of proactive policy: "Canada needs to take deliberate action to maintain control over its economy, or it will become merely a branch plant of someone else's empire."

For my dad, the stakes were not only economic but cultural. He warned that foreign ownership of Canadian media and cultural industries would lead to the erosion of a distinctly Canadian identity. He fiercely defended Canadian content laws and public support for the arts and publishing. In his book *The Vanishing Country*, he warned that Canada could become a "weak, subservient U.S. colony" if it failed to halt the process of Americanization. He argued that this outcome would not be due to Canada's failure to grow but rather its failure to resist pressures that erode its sovereignty and distinct identity.

Moreover, he saw Canada's social programs—especially public healthcare, social welfare, education, and environmental protections—as tied to economic independence. If corporate and political elites prioritized global competitiveness over national well-being, then social policies would be weakened in the name of market efficiency. Today, can anyone argue that he wasn't right?

Canada still has choices. It can strengthen foreign investment review processes, support Canadian industries and manufacture goods here, fund the CBC and the arts, and develop a national economic strategy, in partnership with First Nations and Inuit, that prioritizes Canadian ownership and innovation. But these choices require political will and a renewed commitment to sovereignty.

Listening to the voices of Hurtig and Gordon is not about romanticizing the past. It is about recognizing that the threats they identified—economic domination, cultural assimilation, and political dependency—remain real today. Their legacy is a challenge to this generation: to protect Canada's ability to chart its own course in the world.

Mel once said in a CBC interview: "If you can't, in Canada, create a country which is a great bastion of freedom and opportunity, where you have people living without poverty— if you can't do that in Canada, I doubt very much that it can be done anywhere in the world. We have the wealth and the resources; young and energetic people; space and freedom. It's terribly important that we don't let this drift away so that we find ourselves set on the wrong course and unable to turn back."

That sentiment is at the heart of why we must listen to the economic nationalists who came before us. They foresaw a future in which Canada would lose control of its destiny— first through quiet acquiescence, and then (more recently) by threat of conquest. We cannot let this happen. We do, indeed, have the wealth, the resources, the young and energetic people, and the space and freedom. I suggest we put on our chicken suits and get to work.

The Appointment:
A Short Story

Our appointment was scheduled for the last Friday of the fiscal year. We'd hoped for something sooner. We'd waited a long time, too long, to find out where and when we had to be. We just wanted to get it over with. We worried about what the delay would mean. It's idle time, as much as anything, that can inflame a minor setback into a critical condition, or worse.

For three days we called the office. We left three messages, wondering when a time would be set. There was a lengthy period of anxiety between the news of the campaign, our pending appointment, and when our date was finally confirmed. That time was brutal. It dragged on in a haze of tense ambiguity and despair. We scrolled through the articles and profiles with all of their puzzling images and obscure anecdotes. We had headaches and weren't eating much. We lost weight. Eventually we were informed by automated call. It was finally our time. We made the necessary arrangements and prepared accordingly.

A second, longer message was left in the same cold, digitized voice, outlining the dietary restrictions and any other pre-appointment protocol. We listened and re-listened three times. We wrote everything out by hand on our notepad, underlining the directions we felt were most important.

No solid food, only fluids twenty-four hours before, nothing by mouth the day of the appointment. Not even water. There was a brightly coloured pharmaceutical potion to ingest the night before. We picked it up at the clinic and could tell just from looking at it how revolting it would taste. It was almost glowing.

In bed that night, before the appointment, I asked if he was, like me, scared about tomorrow, about the appointment and what would happen. He had his back to me. I figured he was asleep, and then after a while he said, "It's a part of our shared history. It's common procedure. There's nothing to worry about."

Yet we couldn't sleep. We felt uncomfortable, antsy. We got up. We swallowed two pills, shivering on the fire escape. We got through some of the dishes in the sink. We cut our toenails. We changed the cat's litter box. It was full and disgusting. We sat and listened to the upstairs neighbours arguing.

We went back to bed. We tossed and turned. We tried moving to the floor with our pillows. We kept our eyes closed. Nothing helped. When we did sleep, it was restless, troubled. We had dreams. Bad ones. Dreams about our teeth. Nightmares we hadn't had in years.

You can drop someone, the sick or injured, off at the door, but you can't park there. Not even for a little while. You have to keep going. There's a steady flow of cars moving around the half-circle, dropping off and picking up, like an airport. We have to enter the long-term parking area and walk back to the main entrance.

Even at this hour, the lot is full. There are no spots. Not one. We have to drive into the underground garage, down a steep ramp. The first two levels are full. The first free spot we find is three levels down, 1, 2, 3, under a yellow floodlight that's flickering. It's a tight space. We have to be careful opening the door to avoid hitting the car beside us.

There's no natural light in here; there never is in these dank, depressing lots. No way to tell time. It's always night. We move quickly toward the elevator, ignoring the smell of decomposition, our steps timid, unwilling. We push the button. We hear a shrill horn honk somewhere behind us.

When the elevator doors glide open, we step inside. We push ^. The doors don't close. We push ^ again. We try the "close door" button. We hold our finger on it. It doesn't do anything. We push ^ again and again. Nothing. Just as the doors are finally closing, a hand stops them. A tall, thin man steps into the elevator with us. He's wearing a hat and white surgical mask over his mouth and nose.

Now we're not alone. We all stand in silence, waiting for the doors to close. When they do, it's impossible to tell if we're moving up or down. We stare straight ahead. At one point the man glances at us. He must be very sick. Infected, contagious. We don't want to be here. We don't have to be here. We just want the doors to open.

It's an unbearably slow elevator, maybe the slowest we've ever been on, clattery. While still in disconcerting motion, we suddenly remember we didn't feed the cat. We can't believe we forgot to feed the cat. It's indefensible. We never forget. She will be waiting at her dish, confused, hungry, wondering where her supper is. She doesn't know about the appointment. We told her, but she doesn't understand.

Maybe this man isn't sick. Maybe he's healthy, well. Maybe the mask is for self-preservation, for protection, his armour against outside contamination. Against us.

The elevator stops with a slight lurch. There's an uncomfortable moment before the doors open. The man motions for us to go first. We do, hurriedly, without looking back. It takes a moment to orient ourselves. It's a busy place. There are signs overhead. Some have straight arrows showing the way. Some have arrows that turn at ninety degrees. There are plaques and paintings on the walls. Scenes of nature. There is a gift shop. A café. We want to move. Halfway down the hall, we turn back. The man with the mask is walking behind us.

We're almost struck by a large wheeled cart that's easily seven feet high. It has three levels and is full of clear plastic bags. The man governing the cart doesn't say anything. No sorry or excuse me. *Soiled* is stencilled on the cart.

Ahead of us are two elderly women sitting behind a wide desk. They both have permed greyish white hair and are dressed in matching red vests. A sign above them says *Information*. One of them has a hearing aid. The other has a drooping chin as if she's carved from melted wax. They're laughing and it takes a moment before they notice us. We wave, tell them we're here. They direct us to where we need to be, down the long hall behind them, they say, where we'll find it.

"Find what?" we ask.

"The waiting area," she says.

A phone on the desk rings. The other woman answers it. When we glance back behind us again, the tall man from the elevator is gone.

At the end of a second rambling hall, we turn left into a large room. It's divided into several sections of chairs facing the wall. There's a small TV mounted on the wall in the far corner. On the TV: two shirtless men fighting. Blood pours from a cut above an eye. We all cheer as one. We demand more. More fighting. Less sympathy. The restrained violence isn't enough. The gore benign. The laceration too moderate. To the left of the TV, a set of double doors. We hope we're in the right place.

We flip through a magazine found on a table. One is dedicated to the campaign. The other is a wildlife magazine with photos of birds in flight. We can't believe we didn't feed the cat. No excuse. She's going to be starving without us. She needs us. We put the magazine back down. There's a child sitting at the other end of the waiting room. He's sitting with his mother. We can tell by his eyes and the way his cheeks are streaked that he's been crying. Now he sits quietly. Another cart of bedding rolls by. An announcement is made that we can't decipher.

From our chair, we can see three hand-sanitizer stations. Directly across from us is a row of vending machines, side by side by side. We're looking at the vending machines when a man sits down. Not beside us, one chair over.

He doesn't look at us. We pretend to check out the magazine again. He's holding a piece of gauze to his face, near his mouth. There's a rusty stain on the gauze. It must be a fresh gash. His hair is thinning. No wedding ring. He hasn't shaved in days. His fingernails are long, dirty. He looks pathetic. I'm sure he lives alone. Of course he does. We stand and walk over to the vending machines.

Two for drinks, one for snacks. At the top of the snack machine it says, *Be bright, choose right!* All the snacks inside are identical. Individual spring-loaded compartments with the same candy waiting to be picked. Grey, furry dust balls peek out from under the machines. It should be clean in here. Not like this. Neglected. These are the nooks and crannies they should know about. It shouldn't be left for us to find as we wait for our appointment. We move the dust around with our foot. When we return to our chair, the man with the facial wound is gone. Another is sitting in his place. He shows no signs of trauma or illness. I sit down. I stare ahead.

"For you, or someone else?" he says.

"Pardon?" I say.

"Are you waiting for you, or someone else?"

"Someone else," we say. "We're not even sure we should be here yet."

"I'm only here for me," he says. "I hate these places. But we have to do our duty."

He's holding a small packet in his hands, unwrapping it.

"Would you like some?" he says. "Banana bread. I cut a big enough piece for two. It's good for you."

"That's okay," we say. "Thanks."

"I saw you looking at snacks. None of those are homemade. It's all junk."

"We weren't really looking," we say. "Well, we were looking, *only* looking."

"You have to eat," he says.

"We don't have much of an appetite."

We accept the piece when he passes it to us, and hold it carefully between our thumb and index finger. It's soft and greasy.

"Still warm when I wrapped it," he says.

There are chocolate chips baked in. One of the chips melts onto our thumb. We examine the piece of loaf, both sides, before taking a token bite. We chew longer than we need to before swallowing. We barely have enough saliva to get it down. The wad nearly gets stuck in our throat. Along with banana, there's a vague medicinal flavour.

The man's waiting for a reaction. Before we can say anything, we hear someone. A woman sitting behind a pane of glass, calling out to us.

"We have to go," we say to the man.

We approach the woman behind the glass. She's speaking through a half-open window.

"Excuse me," she says. "Yes, you, you."

"Sorry," we say, looking down, then back to her. "Are we in the right area?"

"You have to fill in these forms first. Don't skip any lines and don't make any mistakes because it's very important. We need all the information."

"So, we're giving you the information?"

"Fill in the forms here, then go to the left and down that hall when you're finished. Follow the signs. Over there. To the right." She motions with her head. Someone calls to her. She turns away to address them.

The forms are on a clipboard. There's a lot of text on the forms. Personal questions. There are many blank lines. It's loud in here. *Be bright, choose right!* it says at the top of the page.

"Do you have a pen?" we ask.

She points to the counter in front of me. There's a pen in a holder. It's attached to the counter with a thin chain.

"You're not supposed to be eating," she says.

"Pardon?" we say. "Oh, it's not ours. Well, it's ours now, but we didn't bring it." We lean in closer to the window. "We didn't even want it. It's his."

"Whose?"

"The guy," we say, turning around. The chairs facing the wall are empty.

"There was a man, and he—" we say.

She cuts us off. "Fill those out," she says. "We need your information."

"Who would ever steal a pen from here?"

She doesn't answer. She's back on her computer, tapping at the keys.

Even before we knew about the appointment, we'd been spending more time at home, hanging around the apartment.

"It's strange," we said to the cat one morning. "No one goes out anymore."

We turned on the old TV out of habit. We'd cancelled our cable subscription so there was nothing on. We missed the soothing diversion of aimless channel surfing. We put on one of the two channels we still had. A local one. The candidate was giving an interview. We fell asleep on the couch. It was a knock on the door that woke us. Loud, aggressive, unending.

We walked to the door slowly. The rapid knocking didn't let up. It intensified. We kept the blanket around us, and opened the door an inch or so. It was her. A woman around our age. She wore a yellow scarf coiled around her neck and face that covered her nose and mouth.

"Hi," she said. "Sorry to bug you. Is it a bad time?"

We'd never met, but we knew it was the girl from upstairs. The unit directly above us. She was wearing a heavy, beige jacket, buttoned up the front. It hung down several inches past her waist.

"Well," we said, turning to look back, "we have some water boiling on the stove."

"It's getting cold out," she said.

"Has the snow started yet?"

"Not yet."

"There's already too much, but they keep saying it's supposed to be this big storm."

"Yeah."

"Storm of the century. Do you need a ride somewhere?" we asked.

We knew she didn't have a car, only a bike, and it wasn't ideal biking conditions, especially on these roads, way out here, away from the city, without any streetlights.

"No, I was out getting some air. I wasn't going anywhere, just biking around for hours. Waiting. What else am I supposed to do? I was on my way back up so just wanted to see how you were doing—you know—how you are?"

"Sorry?"

"I wanted to make sure everything was okay. From last night." She lowered her voice to a whisper. "I could hear you. We have to look out for each other."

What a strange thing to say, we thought. She must have known what we were thinking from our expression.

"Not in a nosy way, just, I see your light on sometimes, at night, late. We're pretty much always home if you need anything."

She pointed straight up with her index finger.

"Even just to talk," she said. "But I don't want to keep you. You should probably sleep now if you can."

That night at dinner we talked about the girl from upstairs, how she had come by before the storm, unannounced. We ate frozen pizza on the couch. We took it out of the oven too soon and it wasn't fully cooked. We were wrapped in the blanket. We didn't think she was worth getting mixed up with. Even then, before the appointment, we already had enough to worry about.

Hours after supper, the lights out, we still weren't tired. We looked under the couch and between the cushions for the remote but couldn't find it. Not that it would have made a difference. There were only two choices, but we didn't like what was on.

We tried to eat a piece of the pizza. We sat up and focused on the TV. "The gap between generosity and depravity," the candidate was saying, "is so much closer than it seems. If you're not careful you might not know which side you're on. Ugliness breeds ugliness. Evil advances evil. That's what we need to fear."

We were still thinking of the girl, of the angry, violent yelling that went on up there most nights, all the fighting. It wasn't healthy. It was scary. We'd heard a door slam earlier, and ever since could only hear one set of footsteps up there. Hers, we assumed, because they were soft and unobtrusive. Then we couldn't hear any at all.

"What matters is family. Living the right way. Taking care of yourself. Nothing else. Look around. Look around you," the candidate said, "and take stock. Immorality is the most destructive sickness and you won't find the cure in anyone else."

After the girl said goodbye, we had closed the door, but kept watching her through the peephole. We'd held our breath. The kettle started whistling from the stove. For the first time we saw her back. From just above her knees to just below her shoulder blades was a wet line of dark brown mud. We knew it was the combination of melted snow, dirt, and salt from her bike's whirling back tire, which was responsible for flinging the dark slush up her back.

Even knowing it was inadvertent and being fully aware the girl was likely oblivious, we felt no better about it. We felt worse. We felt sorry for her. We felt sick to our stomach. She had no idea. From the front, her coat had been so pretty.

We have to lift our feet so the woman with the mop can get at the floor under and around us. Hammering somewhere. A power saw. Work being done. Renovations.

"We can move somewhere else," we say to the woman with the mop. "We're just filling out these forms."

There's a mark on our pants. A stain. Melted chocolate from the banana bread. It looks like blood. We didn't want the banana bread. We never asked for it. It's not ours. We don't need it. We want to throw it out. There's a paper recycling bin, one for plastic, and one for glass. There's no garbage bin. There's nowhere to put trash. We have to pee. We realize we've had to pee for a long time.

We find the bathroom. The door won't lock. This isn't good. We don't want someone walking in. Sometimes the cat walks in on us, but we don't care about that. What if it's a person this time?

The last time we gave a urine sample, it felt so warm in our hand as we carried it to the nurse. We were embarrassed by that overt, obvious warmth. The intimacy of handing it over. There's some graffiti on the wall beside the toilet. Lots of it. Written in different colours. Some is scratched into the paint. Most of it is very small. We have to lean in close to read it. Some of it is unbearably tiny.

Cyclic nucleotide phosphodiesterase of the cardiovascular system Blood platelets Arterial smooth muscle Endothelial cells

There are no instructions on the sample jar, or on the forms. There are lists on these forms that aren't really questions: myocardial infarction, unstable angina, transient ischemic attack. They always have a TV. Always. It's on all the time. They probably never turn it off. There is only one spot to mark an X. We flush the toilet.

"Is that blood?"

"It's just chocolate," we say, covering the stain with a hand. "From the banana bread."

"Do you know where you're going?"

"We're here for an appointment. Our appointment."

"You have that wrong."

"No, we're prepared. We've been preparing for a long time."

"Don't get so worked up. It's for everyone. Not just you. *The* appointment. It's *the* appointment. And the emergency contact is still blank," she says.

"We need a bit more time."

"You're running out of time," she says. "Just mark an X and hand it back."

We hear footsteps. Laughter. Someone is walking this way. It would be better if we could lie down. It would be easier. The paper feels warm in our hand as we pass it back. We should have fed the cat. We try to picture her. Think about her face. But we can't. We don't remember.

"Nocturnal sympathetic nervous system activation. Baroreflex dysfunction. Hypoxia. Hypercapnia."

"What?" we say. "We don't understand. We didn't hear that. What was the last thing you said?"

"Bad circulation. Excessive carbon dioxide. Inadequate respiration. What is the difference between how we view our own moral actions and how we truly behave?"

The air's no good in here. It's hard to see because of the light. It's too bright in here. Why does it have to be so bright? Don't they realize that makes it worse? We don't want the TV on. They should turn it off. It doesn't help anymore. The candidate is still yelling.

"Everything relies on a contingent uncertainty. So much can go wrong," he says. "The worst hasn't happened yet. Trust me. It lies in wait for the vulnerable. True peril is always speculative. Disease is always preceding."

A hand touches our shoulder. A gentle touch, finally. "You should probably sleep now if you can."

But we don't want to sleep. We're trying our best to stay awake, even now.

"Who would ever steal a pen from here?" we ask.

"It's a part of our shared history. It's common procedure," the candidate says. "There's nothing to worry about."

Same Old, Same Old

I'm unsure if you've heard of Dr. Peter Henderson Bryce. He was a significant doctor in Canadian history. In 1884, he wrote Canada's first health code and did some other cool stuff. Then, in 1907, he was asked to inspect Indian Residential Schools in Western Canada and report on their conditions. What he found was horrifying. He clearly documented disturbingly high death rates and provided recommendations that would protect the health of the First Nations students who had been forced to attend these schools. The government's response was not to protect children, but rather its wallet. It suspended funding for Bryce's work and blocked presentations of his findings. They forced him into retirement by 1921.

The government of Canada had a clear opportunity to save the lives of children by acknowledging the deplorable conditions present in the thirty-five residential schools Dr. Bryce studied. Conditions that included overcrowding and poor ventilation. He identified connections between poor sanitation and ill health, which led to a frequent cause of death for Indigenous people: tuberculosis. Not only that, he outed government and church officials as being responsible. Rather than take Dr. Bryce's findings seriously, the government felt its efforts were better placed on ruining a man's career. After all, Indigenous children weren't really children at all, were they? Indigenous children were savages. If you don't believe me, listen to Canada's first prime minister, John A. MacDonald.

When the school is on the reserve the child lives with its parents, who are savages; he is surrounded by savages, and though he may learn to read and write, his habits, and training and mode of thought are Indian. He is simply a savage who can read and write.

Indigenous people were seen as less than human and were given appropriate consideration. That is, little if any. The National Centre for Truth and Reconciliation has documented 4,118 deaths of children, but in 2021 Raymond Frogner, head of archives, anticipated that number will increase fivefold. Approximately 150,000 First Nations children attended Indian Residential Schools. If Frogner is correct, and I believe that he is, that means approximately 20,000 children will have died while attending residential schools. That's 13 per cent.

Since then, every Canadian government has undoubtedly campaigned for change, for the idea that things can and will be different. The most convincing party wins power, and that party has always been Liberal or Conservative.

Over time, most notably in the last decade, Canadians have become increasingly aware of Indian Residential School history and the violent colonial history of this country—how it has profoundly impacted, traumatized, and marginalized Indigenous people and communities. I would like to think that the knowledge Canadians have accrued has affected our collective decision-making process—that what prospective leadership says about the relationship between Canada and Indigenous people matters. For example, that if a new government promises to eliminate boil water advisories in First Nations communities, it will do so. Or at least give it the sincerest old college try.

It was heartening that Canada decided not to vote for Pierre Poilievre. Now, I'm sure that his failure to become prime minister, a position that was right there for the taking, isn't only because he stood by North Island–Powell River candidate Aaron Gunn, who has stated, among other things, that Indigenous bands asked for residential schools. His failure wasn't because he said, "Canada's Aboriginals need to learn the value of hard work more than they need compensation for abuse suffered in residential schools." But I'd like to think it played a significant role.

However, in celebrating Poilievre's defeat in the 2025 federal election, I couldn't help but wonder if it mattered who Canada elected, in terms of how Indigenous people would be treated. I couldn't help but wonder if we have made any progress since 1907, over one hundred years ago. In Mark Carney's acceptance speech, he stated that he planned to work in partnership with Indigenous people. Great! I've heard that promise made before, albeit in different iterations, but maybe it would be different this time. My view of reconciliation has always been that it's about relationships. We need to focus on building community with one another, and isn't that saying the same thing as working in partnership?

Not so fast.

Carney went on to say, quite earnestly, that "humility is also about recognizing that one of the responsibilities of government is to prepare for the worst, not hope for the best." He paused dramatically, concluding that America "wants our land, our resources, our water, our country."

You don't say? That would suck.

Indigenous people across Turtle Island have long experienced the systematic expropriation of their ancestral lands, resources, and water through policies rooted in colonial expansion and exploitation. From the signing of treaties that were often misunderstood and dishonoured, to the forced removals and confinement of communities onto reserves, these actions effectively stripped Indigenous people of their traditional territories and control over vital natural resources. The extraction of minerals, timber, and water for industrial and economic gain further impacted communities, drastically undermining sustainable practices (i.e., never take more than you need from the land, because it only has so much to give) and traditional ways of life. This legacy of resource appropriation has contributed to ongoing socioeconomic challenges and fuelled a continued struggle for reparations and self-determination.

In short, Carney's statement was simply more of what we, as Indigenous people, have been hearing and experiencing for centuries—well before Dr. Bryce was muzzled for speaking the truth, for trying to save the lives of children—and, by all accounts, will be hearing for the foreseeable future, until leadership in this country acts with intention, understands its hypocrisy, acknowledges its past failings, and gets its act together.

Until then, Indigenous people—not Canadians, and certainly not any government—will be preparing for the worst, not hoping for the best. And there are a few reasons for that. The annexation of Canada, through an Indigenous lens, mirrors a historical pattern of land theft. Both involve an imposition of foreign control over territories without consent; these actions have disrupted traditional ways of living, led to community displacement, and allowed for a colonial power to impact us and our sovereignty both historically and in contemporary society. The parallel lies in an injustice: land taken not through mutual agreement but rather domination and disregard for laws and governance. But whether or not Canada maintains its independence (it's likely that it will), we as Indigenous people continue to fight colonial systems: the Indian Act and its framework that undermines self-determination and imposes paternalistic federal control over Indigenous communities; a child welfare system where there are more Indigenous children in "care" today than at the peak of the Indian Residential School system; education and healthcare inequities, where services in Indigenous communities are underfunded and controlled by external governments; and the fact that there are still thirty-eight long-term drinking water advisories in effect across thirty-six First Nations communities in Canada, despite promises made by various Canadian governments. Don't get me wrong, there is hope, but that hope should be placed on younger generations who are learning what Canadians ought to have been learning for decades. It cannot be placed on the promises of white men in positions of power, because they are interested in just that: power, not partnerships.

And there is no humility in that.

DAVID MOSCROP

The Work of Many Years

I'm writing the first words of this chapter in the shadow of Canada's Parliament. Not literally. But close. The buildings are just up the street from where I sit in a coffee shop called Little Victories. The name of the shop seems appropriate. Maybe symbolic. I think most of us would take a little victory right now, the ambiguity of the modifier notwithstanding. A few hundred metres from here, you can see Parliament's famous Centre Block, including the House of Commons, Senate, and Peace Tower. The Centre Block is undergoing major renovations, the work of many years. Much of the area is now a big hole in the ground. I'm trying not to think of that as symbolic, too.

Who knows where Canada's relationship with the United States will be by the time that hole is filled in and the structure is fully renovated. Still fractured, is my guess. It's a pity. Building a relationship between the two countries has also been the work of many years, of many decades, while knocking it down didn't take much time at all. A lot of us feel snakebitten.

I've visited the U.S. more times than I can remember. Today, I refuse to go back. I'm a little surprised at my own refusal. It seems a bit precious. But it's what I think is right. I'm torn, though. If I'd have known this conflict was coming, I'd have driven the California coast one more time or made an extended stop at a New Hampshire Liquor & Wine Outlet.

The work of building a relationship between Canada and the U.S. culminated in a trade agreement worth $1 trillion a year, for better or worse. Getting there was rough. If *Elbows Up!* had been published in the 1980s, at the height of the free trade debate, you'd have a different sort of book. It's ironic, or maybe just twisted, that so much of the 1980s was spent wringing our hands over the threat free trade posed to Canada's culture, identity, economy, and sovereignty. Today, we wring our hands because we might lose free trade. We got used to having it around, branch-plant economy and all.

Along with a lot of trade, we share the world's longest undefended border with the U.S. At least for now. We also share military integration and alliance. We hold deep cultural and personal connections. In many ways, these connections have erased the border in a manner residents of both countries have come to appreciate, a manner that stands in contrast to the literal erasure of the border and the annexation of Canada, the "cherished 51st state," suggested by U.S. president Donald Trump.

It took decades to build the U.S.–Canada relationship, and just months to critically undermine it. The national feeling at this moment is discomfort and distrust, a sideways glance. We'd cross to the other side of the road if we could. Nobody make any sudden moves. Keep your hand on your wallet.

Remember how to form a fist, thumb on the outside. I wish I could go back in time to the War of 1812 and tell the British forces (not Canadian) who burned down the White House, and people living in British North America, where things ended up. I think they'd get a kick out of it. Some might take up the torches again. They'd also probably say "We told you so."

Canadians no longer trust the United States, global hegemon and erstwhile ally. We're looking inward, relaxing rules for domestic trade. Until now, we were quite reliably informed that changing those rules was impossible, as likely as cracking cold fusion. Now, it's easy-peasy. Done by Canada Day. We're also looking outward, toward new or bolstered trade and defence relationships with foreign states that aren't the U.S. That's what discomfort and distrust gets you. But there's more to it, still.

I think if you ask Canadians to use a half-dozen words to describe how they feel about our relationship with the U.S. right now, one of the first few they'd use would be *betrayal*. I think that's the right word. I feel that way. Stabbed in the back, not quite out of nowhere, but the scale of the double-cross is immense.

I feel frustrated, too. And I bet I'm not alone. We can't entirely decouple from America, which is frustrating. We may not want to, which is also frustrating. The U.S. is too big, too close, too convenient, too similar to us for the purposes of facilitating the exchange of goods and services. It's hard to ship things across the ocean to England. It's easier to drive them across a bridge to Michigan. National pride is a powerful force. The path of least resistance is a strong force, too, even after it leads you backwards into a stiletto.

Even with a knife in our backs, we need to keep company with Uncle Sam. Same as it ever was. In the 1968 book *The New Romans: Candid Canadian Opinions of the U.S.*, which inspired this volume, editor Al Purdy argued that the very need for a collection of Canuck hot takes—my term, not his—on the U.S. was because "the most powerful nation on earth is everyone's business, for what happens in the U.S. affects every Canadian." That's more true fifty-seven years later than it was when Purdy clicked and clacked those words on his typewriter. Accepting this means accepting that the relationship between the U.S. and Canada will be fractured, but not ground into dust. At least not any time soon. We'll sit here, frustrated and betrayed, uncomfortable and suspicious, and try to sort it out, personally and collectively, economically and emotionally. But by god we'll try to sort it out.

For me, the U.S.–Canada relationship has an added dimension of some complexity. You'll forgive me, I hope, for using this space for some therapy. I can imagine this book as a lot of things, one of which is therapeutic. For the retail price, it's a bargain.

My father was born in Newfane, New York, in 1962. Newfane is a small town on the south shore of Lake Ontario, just forty-five minutes from Niagara Falls. When he was about two years old or so, my dad was taken from that town and brought across the U.S.–Canada border by his father, without his mother's permission. He was deposited with an aunt from his father's side and her husband. They raised him as their own.

He didn't know until years later that his mother and father weren't his biological parents. He wasn't formally adopted until his late teen years. He never got Canadian citizenship. He never held a passport. Today, we would say he was kidnapped. Perhaps some said as much then, but that didn't change the fact he was taken as a young child from the U.S., from his home, never to see his mother again. He rarely set foot in the country of his birth after that, and never again in his hometown.

For years, my dad's birth mother, Molly, would send him letters and cards for his birthday and at Christmas, a little cash tucked inside along with loving notes. These letters and cards were marked "Return to sender." My dad wouldn't see them. Later in life, as an adult, he learned of their existence. My mother got a hold of them. Molly had sent them to her before she died. She'd hoped my dad would read them, at last. He didn't want to. He couldn't. He was struggling with alcoholism and raising young kids while just a kid himself. He hadn't gone to college or university. He lived in a city, Peterborough, that was heading for the sort of post-industrial decline Bruce Springsteen sang about in the 1980s. That was a decline shared by the rest of Canada and the United States, and one, as it happens, that precipitated Donald Trump, tariffs, our current battle, and this book.

My father's struggle didn't end well. He did later manage to go to college. He became a mechanic. He got sober for more than a decade. Then he relapsed. He drank himself to death in 2014 at the age of fifty-two. Just before he died, he read the letters from his mother. The work of many years.

I've told this story before in private. I've cobbled it together from the information that's been passed along to me from my family. It feels like a story that one should at once never tell and yet must tell. I'm sharing it publicly now because the truth should be on the record. More germane to our purposes, I can't think about the U.S. or explain my feelings about that country without thinking of that story and of my dad. It's a blessing and a curse. I hope he wouldn't mind me sharing all of this with the country at a time when we're sorting out our complicated feelings about our neighbour and—I think I can still say—friend. Cultural and personal connections persist, despite the actions of those who've set in motion the desecration of the relationship.

To betrayal, distrust, and frustration, we can thus add the word *complicated*. From what I can tell, my dad continued to love the U.S. throughout his life, despite his own complicated relationship with the country. He must have watched *Top Gun* a hundred times. I remember seeing it with him at a drive-in. I remember how loud it was, like the jets were overhead. He assembled models of U.S. fighter jets and placed a miniature stealth bomber toy on the dashboard of his red Jetta. He still has that little stealth bomber; it's with him in his burial niche. You don't watch *Top Gun* that often or go to your eternal rest with a miniature American stealth bomber unless you hold on to at least a little fondness for the land of your birth.

For a while, years ago, I considered applying for U.S. citizenship. I didn't research it too deeply. I wasn't sure I was eligible, though I think I am. I have my father's paperwork, vital documents, buried in a box of things I try not to look at too often. I knew that if I applied successfully, I would have to file taxes each year with the Internal Revenue Service. I wasn't interested in that.

It's possible there's more to my dual-citizenship ambivalence. It's possible part of me was motivated to keep away from U.S. citizenship lest I needed to, at some point in the future, go around explaining that I was a dual citizen, as some seem to do for reasons I don't quite understand. It seems almost decadent. Two passports? In this economy? Moreover, I would have had to give up the smug moral superiority, the Canadian national pastime, of judging America and its people from on high. As a dual citizen, would I even be permitted to scoff at the comings and goings and happenings of those who live stateside, saying things like "I can't believe *they* have . . ." I'd be part of them, wouldn't I? Would I have to start apologizing for *my* president? Or saying, "He's not *my* president." *Quelle horreur.* Better to sit in judgment on Jupiter's throne.

I also knew that, if I were to apply for U.S. citizenship, I'd have to confront my father's past, and I wasn't sure how that would go. Writing this chapter and researching Newfane for the first time in years, I recall a trip my dad took our family on to Niagara Falls—the Canadian side—when I was a kid. It occurs to me now, I'm embarrassed to say for the first time, that during the jaunt, he must have thought about his hometown, just over the border, less than an hour by car but decades away. It was a border he couldn't cross, could never cross, whatever the paperwork requirements may have been.

I guess I'm confronting that history now, both privately and quite literally publicly. Writing this is heartbreaking, and I'm starting to regret my choice to do so in a busy coffee shop. If anybody asks, there's something in my eye. Both eyes. Damn Yankees.

But now the decks are clear. You know where I'm coming from—the emotional cobwebs cleared. And you know that, for my part, my feelings about the U.S. are bound up with my father's history. So I'm not a totally honest broker. But I'm aware of it at least, just as I'm aware of my fascination, admiration, revulsion, and hopes for the country Leonard Cohen called "the cradle of the best and of the worst." That line comes from his song "Democracy," and it continues "it's here they got the range, and the machinery for change."

Boy do they ever. For better and for worse. Having travelled throughout much of the northern U.S., having driven across it, having consumed its culture—food, television, film, music, books, video games, architecture—and having studied its history, foreign policy, and domestic politics, I can confirm Cohen was on to something. I can confirm that when Canada loses some or all of its relationship with that place, it's no small loss. For all the trash we can talk about America's past, present, and future (let's be generous and assume it has one), it's a country with its own gravitational pull.

When the Trump tariffs were announced, there was immediate talk of pulling American alcohol off the shelves in Ontario and elsewhere. I supported that move and still do. I also went to buy one last bottle of bourbon before switching to Canadian rye. I'm writing this chapter while wearing a hoodie from Powell's Books, pride of Portland, Oregon. It's the best goddamned place in the world. I could spend a year there. It's the world's largest independent bookshop. It's the size of a city block, its four floors heaving full of new and used books— more than a million of them, in fact. It's like the Library of Alexandria with tote bags.

Here is where I do a little American hagiography, perhaps out of a sense of journalistic fairness and balance, but really just because it's the truth. For years, each American city I visited would become a favourite for its food or architecture or literature or history or whatever. Portland, Seattle, Boston, Chicago, Philadelphia, New York, Los Angeles. I remember driving through the Nebraska grasslands and thinking that land must have been blessed by the most benevolent god. For decades, American sports teams caught my attention. I was a Dallas Cowboys fan and a New York Yankees fan, and not just during the winning years. From grade school onward, I was a Red Wings fan, until just recently, when I gave up the red and white for the red, white, and blue of the Montreal Canadiens—an ironic, colourful twist.

Today, I won't cheer for any American team. Call me petty. But I won't. I don't judge those who do—we all have our reasons for where we draw our lines—but the Trump regime and its enablers have pissed me off sufficiently that I just can't. As I mentioned at the top, I also won't visit any of those American cities I love, nor will I go find new ones to love, any time soon. It wouldn't feel right. Besides, at the rate people are being detained at the border, or worse, I'm one Google search away from finding myself down a hole and without a phone call to my lawyer.

I'm still drawn to the U.S. despite myself. I'm not alone. But I worry the hegemon is in terminal decline. When Robert Prevost, Bob from Chicago, was elected pope and became Leo XIV, Bishop Robert Barron cited the late Cardinal George of Chicago, who said, "Look, until America goes into political decline, there won't be an American pope." America's democratic institutions are falling apart in real time. Maybe it's no longer a democracy at all. The country is run by a lunatic, and it's abandoning the deeply flawed, often violent, but nonetheless core role it played in the decades after the Second World War of cobbling together something of a world order.

What comes next? We don't know. As rotten as much of the American-led domestic and world order has been, it's hard to cheer for chaos, especially since it's at best an even-money bet that something far worse emerges from a moribund America. It's a bit like Canada's complicated relationship with U.S. free trade: you may have hated to adopt it, you may have remained skeptical of it, but when it's gone and you're staring down at a crater in the ground, nobody is celebrating. You start to think it's not the last of the craters to come.

The thing about countries, democracy, and relationships is that they tend to take a long time to build and a short time to tear down. Americans are betraying their own institutions, values, and ideals. It's not the first time. American commitments to what former president Ronald Reagan called the shining city on a hill were always conditional, even hypocritical. The country was founded on Indigenous genocide and chattel slavery. It fought a civil war over the latter, which stands to this day as the bloodiest conflict the country has ever engaged in—and it has never gone long without a conflict. Today, it declines into outright fascism, shredding its own Constitution in the process, a land of immigrants that now disappears immigrants.

As America declines, Canada is stuck working through the feelings that come with having to decide to what degree we wish to, or must, continue our relationship. Even now, our government is discussing joining Trump and company in a zany missile defence scheme, one made all the more uncomfortable by the fact that it might well be an extension of our *existing* relationship under NORAD, a reminder that we're in continental defence together and, by the way, that those nasty missiles, should they one day arrive, will probably be shot down over the true north, strong and free.

Our feelings of betrayal, discomfort, and distrust won't abate any time soon, but neither will a sense that, however much we may need or want to be bound to the U.S., we're profiting from and enabling a country we know to be plumbing the depths of inhumane behaviour at home and abroad. Again, it's not the first time. But we may nonetheless be pressed to answer some tough questions, like just how far we'll go to preserve our own well-being while the world's hegemon, our primary trade and defence partner, swirls around the drain of history and pulls others down with it. So, to the list of feelings, I add guilt.

That's a lot of feelings. Big feelings. Coming to the end of this meandering chapter, I'm reminded that writing is thinking. And I think there's one more feeling to add: grief. It's sad to lose so much of a relationship of the sort Canada and the U.S. have had for so many years—not sure when, or if, you'll fully reconcile, or even want to. I think we're grieving that loss.

Still, the sun breaks through the loss. It's a bright and warm spring day in Ottawa as I write the end to this chapter. Princess Margriet of the Netherlands was meant to be in town to open the Tulip Festival, in recognition of Canada's role in freeing the Dutch from Nazi occupation during the Second World War, but she had to cancel for health reasons. The festival continues and the flowers still bloom. Ottawa is still Ottawa, and we are reliably told by our political leaders it will never be the capital of the 51st state, because Canada is not for sale. That's good news. Most of us prefer not to be American. I think most of us prefer not to be at loggerheads with America, either. Nobody likes feeling distrustful, frustrated, guilty, or betrayed. Nobody likes to grieve.

We may work it all out in time, though. Each generation brings renewal, new approaches, new perspectives, often forgetting or overcoming the past so that they may have a richer future. The Argentine poet Jorge Luis Borges knew how important forgetting was, how crucial it was to survival. He once said, "Forgetting is the only form of forgiveness; it's the only vengeance and the only punishment too." Maybe we'll forget all of this soon, and have our vengeance.

Thinking of that, I wonder what a Canadian looking back on this chapter six decades from now—roughly the same length of time from which I look back on *The New Romans*—will have to say about the U.S.–Canada relationship. I suspect, whatever else may be true of their moment, they'll recognize as familiar the frustrations, anxieties, complexities, and hopes I've expressed here, as they undertake their own work of many years in building a Canada that must exist, for better or worse, alongside the United States. For them, I hope they can build a better, more enduring, more just relationship with the Yankees than we've managed.

For my country, I hope we can protect ourselves—our culture, our workers, our industries, our sovereignty—from

American threats. I hope we can emerge from all of this stronger than when we entered it. My hopes are more modest for myself. I confess a selfish motive here, but I hope our relationship with the U.S. returns to something resembling normal so that I can go back south of the border without guilt or fear. I know where I'll go first. I'll go to Newfane, New York. I'll finish a trip that started with my father in the 1960s, just around the time Al Purdy was setting out to find a handful of Canadians who could express how they felt about Canada's relationship with the United States.

And It's Ours

*I've been hosting Q on CBC Radio for about ten years now, and I've
spent that time very lucky to have a job where I speak to
Canadian musicians and artists, and musicians and artists
from all over the world. But since the threats of annexation
and the "51st state" rhetoric kicked up a few months ago, I'll
admit I've been thinking a little more deeply about our responsibility to share stories about Canadian music, about Canadian
art, and tell the stories of Canadian artists. About the quiet
resistance of making space for the profound art that lives right
here. Reflecting on that made me reflect that I had to fall in
love with the art we make here first.*

I was in Dublin. I was fifteen, so it must've been 2002. I had
flown across the pond for a week of gigs ("gigs" makes it sound
cool—it was more like community theatre performances) with
a Newfoundland fiddle group called the Celtic Fiddlers. Before
you get too impressed: I didn't even play fiddle . . . I played
bass. And also my mom was a chaperone on the trip. But that
week I kept hearing Irish traditional music *everywhere*.
Blasting from the fronts of shops, quietly bleeding out of the

corners of pubs I wasn't old enough to be in, peeking through the crackling speakers of the coach bus while I sat in the back and played Nintendo DS. I was curious about it, so I walked into a record store with the twenty euros I had borrowed from my mom and bought a CD by The Pogues called *The Very Best Of* . . . . I put it in my Discman, pulled on my headphones, and was transported. The music was messy, it was defiant; it had whistles, accordions, drums, *and* banjo. It sounded like it had been written by the smartest person you'd ever found yourself sitting next to at a pub while the bar staff called closing time, or at least what I imagined that was like because again I was fifteen—either way, I didn't know folk music could sound like that. I was in.

I landed back in my hometown of St. John's with a backpack full of Irish folk and punk CDs, and at least two backpacks' worth of the smugness of a teenager who thinks he has found out something cool in Europe. I was all in on Irish music. I even thought about buying one of those flat caps that people wear when they really like craft beer. I showed the CDs to my brother-in-law—who was and is this brilliant musician who had become well known for blurring the lines between Newfoundland tunes and French jazz (I know! Another one of those!)—and he responded kindly but with one small statement that quietly changed my life: *You know we have this stuff here too, right? And it's ours.*

So—contrary to what you might assume from the tourism commercials, not every Newfoundlander grows up dancing arm in arm by a clothesline with his redheaded siblings while someone named Seamus pulls a tin whistle from his wool sock to play an old reel he learned from his grandmother, as we all wait for a Viking ship to dock in our local fjord. I mean *most* of that's true, except for the clothesline. Well, actually, some of us (ahem) grew up in the scenic suburbs of St. John's with grey driveways sprouting grey minivans, rollerblading under grey skies against the blistering wind, throwing fries to grey seagulls in the McDonald's parking lot, and listening to Limp Bizkit and Guns N' Roses on MuchMusic. Wouldn't make a great tourism commercial to be fair, but that was most of my life.

It's funny to think about it now, but even though folk music has been the dominating force in my adult life, I can honestly tell you that, when I was a teenager, I really remember disliking Newfoundland folk music. I was even kind of . . . embarrassed by it.

Here's the thing—to me, Newfoundland music meant the kind of down home music they played on the radio early on weekend mornings, on 99.1 Hits FM and 97.5 K-Rock. They played it every Sunday on shows like *Jigs & Reels* and *Homebrew*, and you'd finish your breakfast and have to wait for it to be over before the "cool" music kicked in. You'd be waiting for 1 p.m., because "What's My Age Again?" might come on, but to get there you'd have to sit through this music with its accordions and fiddles and songs about fishing in a dory, and I'd roll my eyes because it felt like every tune was an oversimplification of who I was, or was the setup to some Newfie joke that someone on the "mainland" was making about us.

After all, I was wearing Led Zeppelin T-shirts and telling myself that good, sophisticated taste didn't include any traditional Newfoundland music. I needed music that felt complex (!), serious (!), soulful (?), and honestly probably American. So I resisted the only way I knew how: I went to Value Village and bought an old suede jacket, flattened my accent a bit on school trips to Toronto (okay, we stayed in Mississauga), and played covers of Cake and The Strokes at the local battle of the bands.

When I tell people this now, people on the mainland will say, "Even Great Big Sea?" Yes, even Great Big Sea! They're easily the most successful group to come out of Newfoundland, ambassadors of our music and culture around the world, but they felt, at the time, kind of . . . I don't know . . . cringey? They were the mainstream, and I wanted music that was alternative, cool, anything but that. Through the (illegal) magic of Napster, I went from radio rock to starting to become obsessed with bluegrass, learned the five-string banjo, and decided all I wanted was to get off the island, move to Tennessee, and play "Rocky Top" on a porch somewhere, and if I had time maybe learn to pilot a steamboat. (I was a weird kid, and no . . . I didn't go on that many dates. I did, however, wear a bowler hat to my prom. True story.)

Okay, so back to what I was talking about: My brother-in-law, as I mentioned, was and is a well-loved and highly regarded musician in Newfoundland and Labrador music circles. I remember when I first met him—he played in bars downtown, he toured, he'd made a CD, he had long hair . . . he was COOL. (Fun fact: he and my sister now make up two-thirds of a Juno Award–winning children's group. Still cool.) So when I got back from Ireland, armed with Irish folk music records, that simple statement of "we have that here too" sparked something in me. He meant: "That Irish folk music you're hearing right now, Newfoundland and Labrador has its own tradition of rich, soulful, complex, serious, and joyful songs, and they're about this place." I immediately started googling articles, went to Fred's Records looking for albums, and for the last few of my teenage years started voraciously researching, reading, and listening to Newfoundland traditional music. I heard the songs and tunes of Tickle Harbour, Figgy Duff, Anita Best, Rufus Guinchard, Émile Benoît, Pius Power, Gerald Campbell, Jim Payne, Kelly Russell . . . the list goes on and on. I heard music that felt powerful, felt urgent, felt like it was my birthright—even though I wouldn't tell anyone I had grown up closer to a Burger King than to anything even resembling a dory.

When I turned nineteen, I started going down to the dark pubs of downtown St. John's, the acoustic guitar I got for Christmas in hand, because I had heard that people my age or not much older got together three or four nights a week for "sessions." I showed up with my dad, sat at the bar and watched for a while, was eventually invited in and found myself in a chair in a circle around a table, playing Newfoundland *and* Irish tunes for hours and hours for the pure joy of it and a few pints. I was taken not just by the musicians' playing, but also the way they talked about the music.

They debated where tunes came from, they shared stories about the players who had carried them along for a while, they laughed about the weird little turns in a melody, they knew raunchy lyrics for some of the tunes that they'd sing in hushed voices so the tourists couldn't hear. They were brilliant. They were sharp. They were so so funny. And they loved and were proud of this music and the culture in a way that totally caught me off guard. I'd spent so long thinking "serious" music had to be brooding, complicated, or found somewhere else—but over the course of a night at Erin's Pub there was lightness and darkness, grief and celebration, heritage and rebellion, a sense of past and a sense of future. All of it, somehow, inside these tunes. Plus it was a great way to drink for cheap.

I started *actively* tuning into the morning radio shows I had once avoided like the plague. Instead of dreading the early hours, I found myself hoping I'd wake up in time to catch some of the Newfoundland music before it stopped at 1 p.m. I started going to the Newfoundland and Labrador Folk Festival and was amazed to see some of my new musical heroes perform live. I would even occasionally get to sit in with them when they showed up at a session. I was in awe of them, but also felt like I was allowed to hold this music for a while too. They answered all my questions, sang all the songs I loved, and were warm and welcoming to a nerdy kid from the suburbs who was way too excited to hear a twelve-verse ballad about a shipwreck.

Eventually, I started a band with my friends. We called ourselves The Dardanelles, and we brought our fiddles, bouzoukis, bodhráns, accordions, and old tunes and songs into the same downtown bars where much cooler indie bands played. We asked the booker of the Ship (the coolest bar in town) to take a risk on us and let us play on a Friday night. We put up posters around the campus and downtown, we put all of our friends on the guest list, and somehow—against all odds—people showed up. The nights we played were filled with students from the university, hippies in long skirts, and hipsters in skinny jeans dancing for hours; they packed the bar, singing along to songs their grandparents might have sung when they were their age, songs we'd only just come to begin to understand ourselves. Even some of our heroes came down to see what the fuss was about. I was completely in love, completely taken, completely at home with the music.

At the time, when people would talk about us as "the next in line of passing down this *important* music," I kept my head down and refused to talk about the "importance" of the music, as I thought focusing on anything but the quality of the music itself might drive people away from it, in the way that I had once stayed away. But of course, looking back now, it *was* important—*to me*. It gave me a language by which to listen to my own home. I started to understand the long history of condescension from the "mainland" toward Newfoundlanders and Labradorians, and how artists like Pat and Joe Byrne, Pamela Morgan, Al Pittman, and Ron Hynes had created music and art that was defiant against any stereotype or mockery but also made unselfconsciously with confidence, power, and purpose. It was music that gave meaning to a generation that had been born Newfoundlanders but had (in 1949) become Canadians.

And, surprise surprise, I went back and listened to Great Big Sea, like *really* listened—and realized (of course) I'd had it all wrong. Here was a band that was massively popular around the world, yet were so deeply rooted in the tradition. They showed up on MuchMusic singing old Newfoundland songs like "Lukey's Boat" and "Wave Over Wave." They started to play massive shows across Canada in front of young, excited, largely inebriated audiences. They wore shorts on stage in the middle of the winter! They were . . . kind of badass? Plus they were generous. They came to our gigs. They invited us to open for them. They helped us make our records. They gave advice we actually listened to—because they'd once been told their music didn't belong on the big stages. But they had kept going, persisting, and in doing so they carved out space for the rest of us coming up behind them, trying to prove that this music, from this place, mattered. Their records were excellent and they deserve to be talked about as one of the not just most popular, but most *important* artists from Newfoundland and Labrador ever.

Eventually, I enrolled in the Folklore Department at Memorial University to study the music and the culture further. Looking back, I do have a lot of compassion for my younger self. Not to say that everyone in Newfoundland *has* to like traditional music, but I do think that that kid who turned his nose up at the music was struggling with something deeper. Maybe mockery from the Canadian media, maybe a kind of cultural self-consciousness shaped by years of being told that "real" art came from somewhere else; that if you wanted to be taken seriously, you had to look past what you were handed. I'd bought into that idea without even realizing it. But after all—what teenager doesn't want to find their own way? And plus I honestly did really like Limp Bizkit, and judging by my top 100 songs from Spotify last year—I still do.

But honestly, and this is an uncomfortable anthology in which to bring this up . . . this newfound patriotism for Newfoundland and Labrador also came with some resentment toward Canada. All of a sudden I was proud that Newfoundland for so many years had resisted Canadian culture turning us into this bland mass. It didn't help that on July 1—while the rest of the country was waving flags for Canada Day—we were observing Memorial Day. And we still do. It's a quiet, solemn day to honour the Newfoundlanders and Labradorians lost in war, especially those who died at Beaumont-Hamel in the Battle of the Somme, where an entire generation was nearly wiped out.

Now, I should be clear . . . not every Newfoundlander feels like I did. Mostly, everyone I knew marked both days. They stood proudly and solemnly at the war memorial in the morning and then went to a barbecue and celebrated Canada in the afternoon. But I was nineteen, dramatic, and full of conviction. So when I turned on CBC TV and saw no mention of how different our days had been, it felt like just another way the country didn't care. I wore T-shirts that said "Free NFLD" and "Newfoundland Republican Army," and still didn't get many dates. It's ironic now to be writing this essay for an anthology about American encroachment on Canada, knowing that I once wanted to stay away from anything "Canada" as much as possible.

Mark Twain once said, "Travel is fatal to prejudice, bigotry, and narrow-mindedness." Sorry for the American reference, but I couldn't find Pierre Berton saying anything like that. Anyway, he and his moustache were right—our band began to travel, and I began to see Canada *very* differently.

The Dardanelles got invited to "mainland" folk festivals in places like Ontario, Manitoba, B.C., and Quebec. We were all between eighteen and maybe twenty years old, armed with our instruments, a pile of songs, and suitcases packed by our parents—ready to take on the rest of the country and show them what the "real" stuff looked like. The shows always went well, and the audiences seemed to like us and would dance and sing—but it wasn't in the festival grounds or during the gigs where the real game-changing moments happened. It was after the shows, in the hotel pubs or lobbies in the dark late hours—after the last act was finished, after the audiences had long gone home and we'd all taken the charter buses back and it was only musicians left. It was then that something would happen. We'd walk into a room with a few scattered hard plastic chairs around a card table, we'd order a few drinks and sit down and start to chat with some of the musicians who were also playing Mariposa, or Shelter Valley, or Summerfolk, or the Vancouver Folk Festival. Soon the instrument cases would be unlatched, and we'd find ourselves with accordion players from Quebec, fiddlers from the Ottawa Valley, banjo players from Manitoba—and over a few (!) pints, we'd hang out, play music, and try to find some common ground. We'd listen to each other's tunes, trade melodies, try to figure out a few tunes we might have in common, have a laugh and talk about where our music came from and what it meant to us. It didn't feel like "cultural diplomacy." It felt like hanging out. And honestly, I think it quietly rewired something in me.

As the festivals got bigger, so did the circles around the table. We found ourselves sitting with Canadian musicians with all sorts of different stories that we didn't often hear in St. John's. We hung backstage and jammed with Inuit throat singers, Métis fiddlers, Ukrainian folk musicians whose families had settled in Manitoba two generations ago, Punjabi musicians playing beautiful tunes on the sarangi who had flown in from their communities in Toronto. There were old-time musicians from Wolfe Island who showed up in bowler hats and suspenders, dressed like it was 1928; Senegalese kora masters who in their later years found themselves living in Vancouver. Weekend after weekend, at every festival a new group of musicians we didn't know—but we'd all hang out around a hotel conference table starting at 11 p.m. and go until the sun came up. There was no audience, no PA, no one asked us to do it—and every night, guaranteed, someone would sing or play something that made me feel a way I had never felt before. Oh, and they listened to us, too. They asked about our tunes and after a few repetitions they played along with our music.

And then the songwriters would show up: Rose Cousins from P.E.I., Alex Cuba from Smithers, B.C., Dan Mangan from Vancouver, Joel Plaskett from Dartmouth, Shane Koyczan from Yellowknife, who with a poem about his family would suddenly hush the room to the point where you could hear the buzzing of the beer fridge in the background.

On some nights, you'd watch two people from seemingly completely different worlds play together for the first time, and then the next morning they'd be on stage together playing those tunes again. I mean, if this was Canadian music, if this was Canada . . . I was all in.

It's worth mentioning that while all of this was happening, social media was taking off—in particular Facebook and Twitter—and in the back of our rented minivan, I'd find myself scrolling and scrolling and reading tweets and posts where I'd be told how I was *supposed* to feel about the rest of the country: Albertans wanted to be Americans (and were full of Newfoundlanders anyway), Quebec didn't like us and wanted to take Labrador, Ontario was full of itself, Saskatchewanians . . . liked wheat? Immigrants, Indigenous peoples, the North—all flattened into headlines or hot takes or early memes. It was rough.

How could anyone feel this way? When you heard someone's story? When you heard their music?

Some of the memories that most stick with me are the late hours where musicians put down their instruments for a second and told me some of the stories of Canada I hadn't learned in school. I remember standing outside a hotel lobby at 1 a.m, sharing a cigarette with an Inuk artist from Iqaluit, who began to tell me how her parents were forcibly moved from their ancestral homes as part of the High Arctic relocation. I remember drinking a pint with a Black singer-songwriter from Montreal who told me stories of the subtle racism they'd experienced over the last few weeks at these so-called welcoming folk festivals we had been playing together. I began to realize that as white musicians from Newfoundland, we came into those rooms with a kind of built-in welcome not everyone received. Around the table one night in Winnipeg, a song from a First Nations group started a conversation about the legacy of residential schools—how even though the schools had closed, the generational trauma continued its destruction.

Sometimes we even found ourselves talking about *us*. Folks who only knew "I'se the B'y" heard us talk about the existential loss that was the cod moratorium, about the starvation-level poverty in rural Newfoundland pre-Confederation, about how some of us *really* felt about those Newfie jokes. One night in particular in Montmagny, Quebec,

I remember some Québécois musicians sat at the table and made these strong, thoughtful arguments *for separatism*. We listened, we chatted a bit about it, we agreed a little then disagreed a little, someone made a joke, then someone else went to the bar to get a round, and then we played music again until the sun began to rise.

I wanted this essay to just be about music but it's worth briefly mentioning how these revelations carried me onto the other paths in my life. On my first CBC radio show, *Deep Roots*, I tried to play Canadian folk music from across the country, partly to show what we might have in common, but mostly because I had learned from these festival experiences that the folk music coming out of this country just *rules*.

And I could see the old "smart versus dumb" binary creeping back into how the CBC and a lot of Canadian media talked about music. The same binary I'd fallen for as a teenager. On one side, there was the stereotype: Canadian folk music as a kind of tweed-jacket nostalgia bomb of greatest hits your parents liked. Fiddles in Cape Breton, jigs from Quebec, sea shanties from the East Coast, "Bud the Spud," Gordon Lightfoot ballads about, I don't know, the railroad, probably?

(Disclaimer: I LOVE ALL THIS MUSIC.)

On the other side, there was the darker, more challenging, experimental edge of folk music—bands from Toronto or Guelph pushing the boundaries of folk into jazz, indie rock, and the avant-garde.

And let's be clear—I loved all of it. Mind you, I started to notice who was getting left out. The traditional groups were left out of the more modern folk festivals, and a lot of those more experimental acts weren't being booked at traditional folk festivals. And those lineups were still *overwhelmingly* white. There were very few artists from Indigenous communities, or from racialized communities anywhere in Canada.

At the same time, inside the folk world, I saw another kind of divide, and saw my privilege in action: older folks would thank us for keeping "real" folk music alive—while we'd get back in the van and throw on hip-hop, or indie rock, or some weird experimental Canadian folk music we'd discovered at another festival the week before. We felt those divisions that had very little to do with listening to music or what we were actually experiencing, musician-to-musician.

And then of course as folk music got cool again, the gatekeepers showed up and there was the backlash to the backlash—the idea that if music sounded even remotely traditional, if it had a fiddle or an accordion or came from a small town, it couldn't possibly be smart, or serious, or alternative, or new.

I knew that wasn't true. I'd seen how deep this music was. I knew how weird and wild and full of life it could be. I knew that most traditional musicians I knew loved more experimental music, and most experimental musicians I knew loved traditional music right back. I knew that oppressive structures aside, musicians just loved other musicians. So part of my goal at the CBC was to push back on that false divide. To play music from across the country—Indigenous, settler, immigrant, urban, rural, traditional, experimental, weird, conventional—and say: *This is all folk and this is all ours.*

I wanted to help open the ears of the Canadian listening public. Or—given that I was on CBC Radio 2 on Saturday afternoons at 3 p.m.—I wanted to help open the ears of a couple of hundred members of the Canadian listening public.

Later, I moved to Toronto to host CBC Radio 2 *Mornings*, and I did that job for about five years. What I learned in that time is a whole other essay, but I do remember, on hearing the burgeoning "Toronto sound" of Drake and The Weeknd, starting to realize these weren't just big hits—they were the sounds of a community that had long been overlooked by the Canadian music industry and by Canadian media (very much including the CBC), finally telling its own story and unapologetically taking over the world.

And when I (somehow) ended up as host of *Q*, the honour and insight of listening to Canadian artists from all different backgrounds only deepened. The stakes have gotten a bit higher in the shadow of the annexation threats, but it's basically the same stuff: getting to know Canadian artists and the stories they want to tell. I'm extremely proud to work with the team of producers on *Q*. I believe they're the best team in radio and podcasting. They are celebrating generational Canadian talent, and always scouting to find who's next, and who has been overlooked. Don't get me wrong, I am extremely proud of the work we've done bringing Canadian art to Canadians, and holding it up next to great art from around the world, but I will admit that since January 2025 I've been thinking about how we can do even more—on radio, TikTok, Instagram, podcasts, YouTube, or the next social media platform, which will probably involve an AI-powered hologram of Rick Campanelli—to create every day a small hour-long encapsulation of that environment I was exposed to backstage at folk festivals: Canadians talking to one another and sharing art as a way to get to know this country and as a way to get to know ourselves. A way of saying, "This is ours."

Listen, I'm no politician. I'm *barely* a journalist. But I think most of us know that we have to learn to listen to one another with compassion and empathy, and I like to think most of us in this country are getting better at that or at least wanting to get better at that. I also think it's hard to know how to begin. Maybe we could take a very small step and start with something a little more literal? Maybe a good beginning would be listening to one other's music, reading one other's books, watching one other's films, going to galleries to see one another's offerings—sitting with the art that comes from someone else's experience of this country. Maybe that's the easiest bridge to empathy and community we have.

To me, that's where understanding at least begins—not in agreement necessarily, but by allowing ourselves through art to feel what someone else has felt and to be moved by what moves them.

And that's what I learned from appreciating the music of my home and then the music of this country; it's what I've learned again and again in my time on CBC Radio: that listening—deep, real, attentive listening—is the foundation of connection. It will be at least part of what holds us together when our sovereignty is under threat. Sometimes the first step is to listen to a different kind of song.

CANISIA LUBRIN

Never Leave and the Leaving Is Easy

Sometimes, one must begin by putting things away. The idea of The Nation State™ as the supreme, all-encompassing, absolute, and protective definition of collective belonging, for example. Because it is the result of joint assaults of a history of supremacist ideologies and the complete triumph of political disorder over the well-being of the earth's inhabitants. Only in the paradigm of The Nation State™ does *person* become resident and citizen, and therefore subject to a system of values that is based less on life, justice, and truth than on scarcity, exclusion, and suspicion. The human is a nomadic—or, at least, a portable and roaming—being.

The stories of the world make the most sense when illuminated by the structures and conditions of human movement. Whether, as human history shows, this movement is voluntary or by capture, there is language inside of which writers and storytellers are the exposure at the root of nearly every form of memory. With the emergence of games of empire, colonialism, capitalism and its twin sibling, chemical warfare,

The Nation State™ came to supersede the organic and truly communal forms of sociality that caused human beings to (wait for it) . . . move about the globe as necessary for survival and thriving. Further still, to leave records about it all. Many so durable, in fact, that they've become the foundation of entire schemes of political, philosophical, and religious thought, on which billions of people mount their whole lives and deaths. How else to know in the early twenty-first century what went on in ancient Mesopotamia, Ethiopia, Greece, Peru, Turtle Island? This is not to say those eras were perfect times. No time is. But I engage in such naming of places to acknowledge that more is at stake in the present world than the history of nationalism imparts. Whatever internal contradictions existed in those earlier attempts at shared living could also have been based on systems far more reciprocal than the one in which an elite minority appropriates every sphere of public—and even private—life in order to hoard more and more of the world's resources and wealth.

There is little doubt that the conscription of all planetary life into the balance sheets of one economic structure (The Nation State™) is as reductive and destructive a form of management as you can hope to have for an ecosystem as complex as planet earth's. So, a first step to understanding geographic invasion and land seizure is to reckon with the context of the historical time of imperial conquest in whose cultural, political, and scholarly cauldron we still live. In this way, the nation is sponsored by the ruin of those more ethical practices and ideas based on genuine care and stewardship. To be protectionist about the window-dressing sovereignty of the nation is to also be bound to transformations still to be realized of the value of human and non-human life here. But we live in a capitalist time, and more than any other time, it is rife with anti-intellectual ⚖.

The old anti-intellectual balloons have ✳ in some weird ways, because certain technologies, like the internet and social media, have been put to captive, manipulative, and other dangerous uses. Though, to be generous to their originators, these tools were likely not conceived to doom the development of critical thought. If social media can be a case study: among its numbered benefits, it is primarily an arena where too many people globally are loud and wrong together, until, mercifully, the opposite might hold for an hour in the world. Until you also realize the thing you've been calling a person is a bot, or thousands of bots. It's a place of endless tussle about important things, but with a limited grasp of them. The simulacra don't dull the sting of the fighting or the general sense of injustice that enters the cybersphere. The scale of our malcontent is at its widest today, and we have nowhere useful to express it but the internet. Not even when the representatives of the nation promise they hear us every election cycle.

It used to be just three guys with watered-down whisky by the road or in the town hall talking occasional sense and mostly nonsense on the hi-fi. You could note them, or you could join them with quibbles of your own, or you could carry on with your day where there was a garden to tend, a roadside to clean, a meal to prepare, and a friend to laugh with as you moved at your own pace. But now, a Tweet, a TikTok, or a Thread can spell systems-wide disaster for public perception and even policy (see: George Floyd, The Middle East™, and any number of conspiracy theories linked to the peak of the

COVID-19 pandemic), or swing the opposite way. This unfiltered, uncontrollable tool controls and influences more than a responsible and mature public should tolerate. But no one's promised a mature humanity online. What exactly is the nation in such a world today? It is nothing more than a managerial toolkit for the most powerful to administer the world's resources.

This toolkit is why the entire sham of political democracy has taken hold everywhere. It is why the president of the most powerful nation in the world, Donald J. Trump, can simply announce on a regular, regular Tuesday in February, mere weeks after his inauguration—while you are having dinner and many others are starving, suffering bombardment and slaughter, irrationally imprisoned, intentionally poisoned, and refused care—that he'd love for his country to extend its borders to include one of the most resourced Nation States™ in the world: Canada. And, of course, why not take Greenland as the litmus test. Suffice to say that neither country marked for border absorption—one the small brother next door, the other an "ally" a whole continent away—was amused. What littered the internet in the following days was evidence that a substantial percentage of Canadians and Americans had suddenly come to see the fickleness, if not the downright illusion, of Nation State Safety™ in its truer guise—what it upholds as its raison d'être being not primarily the well-being of its populations, but the morbid playground of a profoundly corrupt ruling order. Who could have predicted so many instances of *we're sorry, Canada, please don't stop fighting* posted online by folks in the neighbouring centre of empire, so early into a presidential term that had already promised jarring moves to authoritarian rule. Many of us who've been paying attention to the history of colonialism knew that threats of annexation would soon follow. And follow they have. The Nation State™ is that big chamber of unnatural things bound to a naturalized paradigm of living beings. Revolution is revolution for this reason.

Lest I be accused of romanticizing the foibles of a world without all the gains we've manoeuvred since this form of arranging life on this planet was invented, or without the servile successes of modernity, consider what is innate and what is incidental in this theory. The Nation State™ was, is, and has come to mean everything about how the world is meant to behave toward capital, its centers and its storehouses, and therefore to those who hoard the most of it. Which is through morbid obedience, which is punitive acquiescence, which is speed, speed, speed through something called work and the (re)paying of lifelong, crippling debt. The expressway, the bank, and the stock exchange are the nation's triangle pillars, and these have widened the gap of inequity to such a margin that what most people have in the way of social connection is the dating app, the social network, the streaming platform, the endless lectures about banning plastic straws to save the sea turtles. In The First World™, the world's Chief Economic Exploiter, it is ordinary to live among others you call neighbour whom you see three times per year, sometimes when there's a holiday. Even those to whom you've never uttered a single word. And you must pass through open season on the crosswalk with police dressed in four kinds of metal, there to protect a bronze bull in the same place where millions go hungry, while food waste by the millions of kilograms per day is another affordance of tax breaks for the already-too-wealthy. And you walk through your door and open an app that comes with a pre-set button for the world. And its carbon trails are mostly hidden from your view, a network of electronic footprints requiring massive water reserves to cool its centres. And the monied class which itself defies every category of the nation to which a permanent underclass must adhere, they assume your neck of the woods to be the next location for their endless expansionist doctrines. And soon online becomes fuel for the ranting, the doling out of frustrations, the easy answers to the desires of the flesh. And you wonder about some things:

» The meditative moment between thought and action
» The break, if holding the break balances the claw on your own neck
» What is really going on with the many people you've "friended" in the cyberspace
» Why so many people praise, defend, and treat as sacrosanct this state of affairs
» Colours shapes forms aesthetics of living this "life"
» A break from ordinary form
» A break from everything else

⟶   ⟵

Capitalist fever dreams infect every sphere of public, spiritual, and political life. The simultaneous laboratory and limbo of ecological catastrophe, political artlessness, fatally regressive propaganda, the censorship of history, and geopolitical chaos. How these can erase decades of experience and learning and keep naïveté solid.

⟶   ⟵

In this is a challenge to the curiosity it takes to relearn the world. It is the imagination of resilience and critical thinking that can survive the deliberate warping of reality that these architects of corrupt knowledge systems manufacture. The coopting of journalism, the playbooks of a degraded political class, all of the levers that an unethical and very monied ruling class can pull to control peoples the world over by attempting to rewrite history with the unimaginably cruel tyrannies they program into our lives. They present these measures as reasonable, necessary—and even good—and with such sweeping authority that genocide, slavery, indentureship, climate calamity, ecocide, and annexation are upheld inside of legal structures. And inside of that atmosphere, we are left bereft, meaning itself is trampled on, rearranged, and turned into an oppressive force, a tool for further exploiting the world.

Literature as I imagine it, during times of such catastrophe, is important for clarifying our relation to this world and self. It is a crucial depository against erasing the presence of those whose lives challenge the domination of such systems. It offers another set of presences—language that underscores what it means to care deeply and to encourage fuller humanity. This might be an antidote to the delusions of a culture with no deep memory of its past. One in which storytellers who recognize the integrity of this work—targeted and wiped out (even through banned books)—are an important part of the unbearable cost in societies where the only surviving account of *being* and life becomes the tyrant's.

But what is literature for, they say. Isn't art merely for art's sake, they say. As though the sake of art were neutral in a world as vastly unequal as ours. I am suggesting instead that literature is vast enough to be instrumentalized in nearly any direction. And that is something to both respect and to regard with some skepticism. Even as my trust in literature and the imagination is now at its most potent that I can remember. The multiple genocides underway, the record-shattering hurricanes, the tribal wars, the pretence to democracy, forest fires ruinous enough to destroy entire communities, floods large enough to bury whole neighbourhoods and towns, migrants stranded on rough seas and at ports and borders across the western world, because the effects of colonialism called "environmental and economic crisis." All because these call to deepen the work of imagining other ways to support living with an ethics of care. Literature, then, could be a way to turn away, to escape, but it is also readily weighted from this one vestige of possible life. So, I pick up a pen against the possibility of collective death and amnesia, not toward fortifying anything called The Nation State™.

But I am not naive about what literature can do at this hour in the world. Writers are a link in a series of catastrophic times on earth. The novel I write won't cure famine for the millions who hunger. The story I have written won't stop a genocide, or a war, or quell the rumours of wars bubbling up everywhere. The poem I will write won't stop the sea levels from rising. But they are a record, a witness, an account of what it means to face the peril, and ultimately to be in relation. These can bring us into proximity. In such a way, we might be available to each other's needs and wants and visions. Writing might incite some act to risk for betterment, to enact a different kind of regard, on the world, and on each other. It can orient us to each other's meanings, to each other's expressions, and to each other's way of living.

If literature is one of the most multi-part and vast forms of sharing imagining, literature can then mean to transform, to change minds, to have as vast a range of visions as possible in the important dialogues concerning art, and our lives beyond art, and boundaries drawn around our lives, including The Nation State™. Who desires a world beyond a given solipsism that literature can't impress upon? Perhaps the membrane between cultures and nations and differing norms has always been this porous.

In 2018, a year after my first book (*Voodoo Hypothesis*) was released, I was accepted into a mentorship program for marginalized writers at the Banff Centre, where I would work among peers on a novel I started writing in 2012. Knowing something of my predecessors and realizing I knew no Black Canadian novelists who were my immediate peers (women under forty), I was curious who else found this gap important. So, I posted a query to Facebook, where I had some 3,000+ "friends."

The reasons for this curiosity are manifold and obvious, one would think. Yet, in a long, perhaps 130-response thread, in which no one could name a single Black woman novelist under forty writing contemporary "Canadian Literature," I was accused of being ageist, and a few people wondered why I would be this specific, and what was I trying to say about good ole Canada, anyway? Most responses, however, were filled with shock and dismay at what was obviously a legitimate form of cultural exclusion faced by Black Canadians, not to mention those with any desire to make literature. This was eight years after I first started to submit my work to magazines—with the first four years returning 100 per cent rejections—and (remember) three years after the editor, visual artist, and poet Paul Vermeersch acquired (by 2015) *Voodoo Hypothesis* for Buckrider Books. I had my first three magazine acceptances that same year. Remember: 2018 was three years after #OscarsSoWhite, and two years before the public execution of George Floyd in 2020 opened the flood-gates for #PublishingSoWhite. The history of art is also a history with its own damning narratives.

Over a decade ago, David Chariandy stated that Black Canadian literature "is now an established term" and noted its "protracted and complicated emergence." And whether we can say the awareness that has led to this is new or not, there is that two-hundred-year-old history of Black writing here behind us. It is both enabling and limiting if the keepers of the gates rely on algorithms that replicate and protect historically homogenous views of the world and its cultures. No one wants to live in a culture with no memory of their existence.

It is not only important to know that Black Canadian liter-ature appears to be firmly established both as a discipline and in the public imaginary. Black Canadian writing's well-documented two-hundred-year-old history includes a broad range of literary cultural production, theory, cultural activism, and archival documents. But here I was in 2018 wondering where the Canadian women writers under forty were, because I was and am interested in our cultural knowledge and in our wider dialogues, and in the breadth of the imaginations we engage.

By now, of course, high-status literary prizes such as the (recently embattled) Griffin Poetry Prize, Trillium Book Award,

Writers' Trust prizes, Danuta Gleed Literary Award, the now-embattled Giller, and GGs have been awarded to notable Black Canadian authors such as Dionne Brand, Esi Edugyan, André Alexis, Téa Mutonji, Suzette Mayr, Zalika Reid-Benta, and Kaie Kellough, among others. Not only can I now name my immediate peers—a thankfully, growing group—I co-edited *The Journey Prize 33* along with David Chariandy and Esi Edugyan, which featured ten stories written by Black emerging writers. I can name my peers without the concentration a person might need to solve complex questions about the atomic universe: shout-out Téa Mutonji, Zalika Reid-Benta, Christina Cooke, Rebecca Fisseha, Djamila Ibrahim, Iryn Tushabe, Zilla Jones, Jasmine Sealy, Francesca Ekwuyasi, Juliane Okot Bitek, and others—and that's just the women. Novelists, short story writers, poets, memoirists—with published or forthcoming works. Yet, it is still true that while Black Canadian literature as a discourse is recognized, its relationship to institutions, critics, and students of Canadian Literature remains tenuous. So, the "absented presence" that Rinaldo Walcott names in the treatment of Black artists in Canada might well be a present concern even with these improvements.

I attempt here to think more concretely about the history of these deadly delusions of race, power, and capital that colonialism spread across the world, which influences too many forms of cultural production, even when they suppose oblivion. In this way it is impossible not to scrutinize the forms of literature that undergird such a blueprint. One that stretches from continent to continent, and in fact overlays the contemporary global condition of late capitalism where empire continues its conquests, even invisibly. And so, the attempt to draw reason from this will inevitably dissolve at a certain point. The making of a literary establishment that believes itself the absolute progeny of ancient Greece and Rome lies in that summation. One could read such historical accounts and think, perhaps naively, that bygone cultures and societies are the cautionary tale of what supremacy at its peak can do, of the rifts of caste and class, of hierarchy and the morbid passions of estheticizing any form of human superiority. But to be aware in this world is to be endlessly attuned to the ways that chronologies dissolve and histories intermingle and disrupt our sense of time. In this way, the literature of the underclasses does name the seemingly never-ending litany that attempts to repair the gaps in our cultural memory. Who else will represent the people than the people themselves? The people who have lived the impossible horror and wonder that amount to their lives. I say "impossible" here to avoid trivializing what is already routine. I am interested in the role of language in this form of world-making, and so I come to think about the work of the writer as a keeper of memory, as a cultural custodian. What the writer does, who the writer is able to sound like, why the writer depends on an authority to speak for and of life. Sylvia Wynter states in her 1971 text "Novel and History, Plot and Plantation" that "the novel form and our societies are twin children of the same parents." Libraries and even more (para)cultural institutions that have spread into the twenty-first century are overfull with such evidence, with the continuing expressions of who we are inside and beyond the accepted definitions of The Nation State™.

Here, I am most concerned with how the least powerful are impacted by the stories that get told or otherwise do not get told. The perils of a culture with no true memory of itself, or only a partial one. Or, worse, one in which what is true is replaced by the pompous delusions of the ruling order.

Now, I didn't come here to frighten you. Storytellers did this work with the voice, with pictures on rock, before the invention of paper. Storytellers found more ways to do this with the invention of pottery, with paper. And even more ways to do this because of the invention of the printing press. And writers gained even more ways to do this with the invention of the telegraph, the stereograph, the monograph, the internet; and storytellers may well keep doing this through the eras and eons of the world's evolving technologies, theatres of imagination and manipulation, of war and dissolution, and through any of the imaginaries of wonder and disaster our species has the capacity to create.

Without storytellers, we'd live in a cultural void. Memory, as imperfect as it is, suggests lineage, being, history, as much as forms, aesthetics, and structures that legitimize the social function of imagination. Of art and the ways that it asserts our freedoms and dignities.

A people should not have to request their existence be respected, acknowledged, and affirmed. To participate in the forms of worlding that literature calls into being is to have full participation in one's complete humanity, whether or not it is legible in the registers of The Nation State™.

And yet, far too many of us must ceaselessly justify our desire for this participation, this sovereignty. Too many of us must still be monitored with whatever logic determines what stories by "the others" are worth acquiring, editing, publishing, distributing, promoting, and discussing. And heaven forbid if it doesn't make (money) sense to "America."

It is in the absence of such regard that extremist ideology develops. The extremism is in denying people their inherent freedoms and dignities, even in terms of how to express themselves with art. By proxy: to live fully.

When we say no to those who would abuse the limits of their own freedom and power, we are merely intervening for the sake of our being. If we say no, it is because we have been forced to act against those who do not respect our being. Those who disagree with our existence. Those freedoms and dignities that exist beyond the corrupting impact of rights, laws, privileges, decrees, doctrines, and directives from centres of structural and systemic power, where the possible opposite effects of rights, laws, privileges, decrees, and doctrines hardly have a chance to bloom for long.

Those corrupt actors who choose to act only to deepen their assertion of power both claim and accept ignorance as their own organizing process and principle. The logic is, *well, if I didn't know then I can't be blamed*. Ignorance is, of course, one of the most dangerous forms of knowledge. It is unknowledge that can be wielded to exclude, to destroy, to protect, to enact, and at once place exculpatory veils on the senses. It is a blunt instrument. It works simply. Count, for instance, how many times by May 1, 2025, the forty-seventh President of the United States of America replied to press questions about the havoc caused by his executive orders with "I don't know anything about it," and for this response to simply have sufficed for the journalists in the room, those who themselves have been silenced in exchange for access, or who are complicit. We risk living in a culture with no memory, if the ideas that inform the establishment's whims are the same ones that exclude the courageous and critical voices on the margins from the podium during times of large-scale crisis. It is discomfiting but necessary work to write, acquire, edit, publish, and distribute works of literature that face peril and do not merely take interest in the comfort of the powerful.

Likely, if a culture with no memory serves you, you detest that there is new (to you) knowledge; that whatever has made your memory easy no longer suffices.

Maybe this is what it means to speak every language poorly. To know our lives are dramatic. To live in a time where everything is exaggerated and low-key. Our joy, our sorrow. And we joy sorrow. And we worry joy. And everything is dismissed. Our joy. Your sorrow. And I admit: I am not original in anything. But I like to believe I'm personal. To think, truly think of what it takes for anyone to be free to move as needed to survive (in the world, as in the imagination) is to think of everyone with the weight of invasion held over their lives. And I promise myself in all this, I can write. The only thing human to do is press against mortality, to refuse—after Thomas—a gentle going into that good night.

It is important to insist that the culture remembers and is remembered. There could be silence between the shore and the boat in a world almost completely underwater. Rounds and rounds of our peoples covered in the dirt of our world. And we'd need to remember and hope to make better judgements in the future, even into a future that is unclear.

Why should a long line of people walking on the surfaces of the earth for miles and miles, begging or mute before guards with service dogs angled at children buried under rubble—why should they have to teach us anything about their humanity for us to observe and remember them as fully human? And yet the stories we tell in that hard becoming often outlast us. Another day will break again from the edge of a smoke-heaving forest with us ogling page after page, searching for generous evidence of human encounters there. And nothing called The Nation State™ can speak because it never had a mouth or a heart, other than your ventriloquizing.

Whether you saw a bird standing yesterday on the sail of a catamaran belonging to the world's youngest and richest man, or—one hundred years from now—if you can imagine your descendant reminding her friend that, once in the past, a robber Barron had somebody scrub his memoirs of the account that accurately drew his portrait with the 99 per cent of spilled blood his empire used to secure the kingdom for his progeny. One day—because he had the power to tell that story, false or not—your descendant can point to an archive of your stories and say, look, there is one more chapter in which you are more than the account of an oppressive history. Your descendants come from more than just a conquered people . . .

This is what it means to resist living in a culture with no memory.

And it might be easier, then, to imagine the same news of this same nightmare of hard times we are living. The graph of remembering can sprout from every skull. Who—in such a vision—can make no mention of having written any fictions on earth? The stories of such a history are less likely to be sanitized because things are remembered, and nothing needs to be pure.

· · ·

The things culture reveals best are our desires. How desire can swallow decades of experience and keep naïveté solid. And culture, too, is a form of power that must always be scrutinized for rot. Even and especially of the self-fulfilling kind. A fool familiar with the dictionary is still a fool with too much to say. And who should listen to folly begging folly? So, I've written this note, also to remind myself of these things. And now it ends with one of the many thousands of theories about who or what the writer is, about what writing does or should do, and about the means, structures, and genres existing in the value systems that replicate them.

If literature is to comment on the forces that order meaning in language, if art's philosophical keystones are concerned with questions, then such questions are implicated in the health of the places in which we live. Art-making, we presume, is that arena of conflict, happenstance, divergence, and study. It can open the full range of human emotion into extreme imaginative tests. It can be formed by interweaving many radical, discipline-exceeding parts. If the possibilities for art-making involve practices that both limit and enlarge the imagination, it is in art's many wounding subjects that "the human" as a narrative project remains volatile. And so, it is important not to idealize the writer. Ever. Just as you should not idealize The Nation State™.

The writer, then, is a hypothesis that can measure itself against such questions. What braces up literary creativity and the readability of the imaginative act, on the other hand, is the hypothetical, world-orienting excesses of the more-than-human. As though all of our lives can depend on one beloved who will stand behind us and speak the thing we need to hear: that there is no finish here, there is only a run of choices we can make, and they have such interesting lives after we make them; they can live as water, as pigment, as copper and feather and steel in our stories, sculptures, pictures, movies, poems, and plays. The new sounds we can make, the new abilities for duration we develop, the enchantments like rivers held taut and true all along our lives. We continue. Time, exceeds. Taste and perception, re-evaluated.

Writers persist against the precarity of living memory. And literature depends on the miscellany of the world as much as the deep wells of human experience from which lives are made and unmade. When done well, it keeps to one of the primary functions of art, which is transcendence. Such an invitation can only be hard-won, deeply fraught, and puzzled by as vast a range of human concerns as any of us might imagine a writer could bring.

In a notebook somewhere I drew line-like figures—gathered—all from my own memory of this world. A world if it were diffuse, porous ground—but one which I am aware we cannot have the same memory of, even though the sensuous instruments of our bodies are similar. In literature, we can choose to lose the mask of the universal and its romances with sameness, in favour of revelation, coexistence, and difference.

If I admit that today I've seen the generosity of a different space with you here, one that agrees everything can stretch to hold us all when the membranes between our lives are soft, imagine then what could we carry, moving like that through our dramas, our lives, our clusters, and the stern world that teaches us to be wild, to be imperfect and available to improvement? It cannot be The Nation State™, which holds itself as complete and absolute.

Such otherwise visions I find on my own shelves: the plural undertakings that reveal and enrich life.

I say thank you to the writers who invite me into the materials of their memory and experience. And I would be lucky to find such abundance there. Because things begin to happen at the very edge of a life where to open as one thing and end as another means you have walked into a room filled with the art of a person and there you might find a treatise on forgetting the world (surviving past the disasters of this colonial time).

KEN DRYDEN

The Atlantic Online (February 2025)

Canada Is Taking Trump Seriously and Personally

Last Saturday, I was in Montreal for the Canada–U.S. hockey game in the 4 Nations tournament. I knew I needed to be there. A few nights later, I was at home in front of our TV for the final game, which Canada won 3–2 in overtime. I watched every moment, from before the game began to after it ended. I almost never do that. Those games, I knew, were going to say something—about Canadian players, about Canadian fans, about Canada. Maybe something about the United States too. I didn't know what.

Sports can tell big stories. I was one of two goalies for Canada in the Canada–Soviet Union series in 1972, the first international best-against-best hockey series. Until that moment, professional players from the NHL were not eligible to compete in the amateurs-only Olympic Games or World Championships. Canada was where hockey originated, where all of the best players in the world were born and developed.

To the total annoyance of Canadians, year after year the Soviet Union, not Canada, became known as "World Champions."

The 1972 showdown was eight games: four in Canada, four in Moscow. Everyone—the Canadian players and fans, even the Soviet players and fans, and the experts from both countries— knew that Canada would win decisively, likely all eight games and by big scores.

In Game 1 in Montreal, the Soviets won, 7–3. Imagine the reaction all across Canada. Then multiply that by ten.

Instantly, the stakes changed. Something deeper than hockey pride was on the line. We were the best in the world when it came to hockey; the rest of the world didn't think about Canada that way when it came to many other things. Now we had lost. What did that say about us? About Canada? About Canadians? The next seven games would decide. These were the stakes.

We left Canada trailing two games to one, with one game tied. We lost the first game in Moscow. The series was all but over. Then we won the next two games, leaving it to one final game. In 1972, not many North Americans travelled to Europe; almost none went to Moscow. Three thousand Canadians were in that arena. They were there because, somehow, they knew they had to be there. For the last game, on a Thursday, played entirely during work and school hours all across the country, 16 million out of Canada's population of 22 million people watched. Behind two goals to start the third period, we tied the game, then won it, and the series, with thirty-four seconds remaining. I felt immense excitement. I felt even more immense relief. In that series, Canadians discovered a depth of feeling for their country that they hadn't known was there.

In 1980, I was the other person in the Olympics booth in Lake Placid, New York, when the U.S. beat the Soviets and later won the gold medal. (When Al Michaels said, "Do you believe in miracles?" "Yes!" I said, "Unbelievable.") At the beginning of the Olympics, for the U.S., there were no stakes. The team was made up almost entirely of college kids. The Soviets, at the time, were the best team in the world. Even after the U.S. team won some early games, their players seemed on a roll to enjoy, not to be taken seriously. Then they beat the Soviets and two days later defeated Finland to win the gold.

This was not a good time for the U.S. in the world. Among other problems and conflicts, Iran was holding fifty-two Americans hostage in Tehran. Weeks passed. The U.S. seemed powerless to get them back. Unbeknownst to all but a few, six of the hostages—all American diplomats—had escaped and were being hidden in the Canadian embassy. The Canadians sheltered the diplomats for months, and eventually helped them escape. The news that the diplomats had made it safely out of Iran came just before the Lake Placid games began. Everywhere I went around the village, Americans came up to me and said, "Thank you, Canada," as if they were otherwise friendless in the world.

In 1980, hockey was not a major sport in the U.S., and so Americans had no expectation or even hope of winning against the Soviets. What they did have at stake in 1980 was the Cold War. That they had to win. The hockey team's victory in Lake Placid felt like part of this bigger fight. It fit the story Americans wanted to tell about themselves. And although hockey was a fairly minor sport, forty-five years later, for many

Americans, the "Miracle on Ice" remains their favorite patriotic sports moment.

Now to today. Now to the 4 Nations tournament. Being Canadian these past few months hasn't been a lot of fun. The threat and now the coming reality of high tariffs on Canadian goods exported to the U.S.—and the disruptions and dislocations, known and unknown, that these tariffs will cause— is never out of mind. Even more difficult in the day-to-day is Donald Trump's relentless and insulting commentary.

Canada as the U.S.'s "51st state"; Prime Minister Justin Trudeau as "Governor Trudeau"; the U.S. using "economic force" to annex Canada, its nearest ally and inescapable geographical fact of life. It's the kind of trolling that Trump does to everyone, to every country, whenever he wants to, because as president of the most powerful nation on earth, he knows he can. He loves to watch the weak wobble and cringe, and those who think they're strong discover they're not.

Na na na na na. It sets a tone. It lets everyone know who's boss. It's what he did all his life in business. And although at a boardroom table he wasn't always the guy with the deepest pockets, in the Oval Office of the United States of America, he knows he is. Being Donald Trump got him elected, but being president is what allows him to be Donald Trump. On November 5, nobody had as much at stake in the election's result as he did. He needed to win to hold the world's highest office, to avoid lawsuits and prison time. He needed to win to be him.

It's been amazing to watch world leaders of proud, historically significant countries, kings in their own domain, suck up to Donald Trump, to see billionaires and business titans, who know how the game is played—cater to political authority in public, play hardball in private—who reside proudly and smugly above and beyond politics, fold like a cheap suit. And later, when they do respond, because prime ministers, presidents, and CEOs eventually have to say something, their words sound so lame. "There's not a snowball's chance in hell that Canada would become part of the United States," Trudeau said. By answering at all, you end up making any slur sound slightly, disturbingly legitimate, and you make yourself look weak.

How would Americans react if a president or prime minister of another country said the same about their president? That he's *crooked*, *crazy*, a *lunatic*, a *loser*? That he's the worst president in the history of the world? That their country is just another failed empire in its final death throes? That both president and country are a disgrace and everyone knows it? Probably not well.

But what do you do? What do the decision-makers in other countries do? What do average Canadians, average Panamanians and Danes, what do ordinary people anywhere do? That's why I needed to be at that game in Montreal.

Thirty years earlier, in 1995, on the weekend before Quebec's second referendum on independence, my family and I went to Montreal to wander the city, to try to sense what Quebecers were feeling, but mostly just to be there. On the Saturday night, we went to a Montreal Canadiens game. We wanted to be there for the singing of "O Canada." The next day, a reporter for an English-language newspaper wrote that it was the loudest he had ever heard the anthem sung at a game. What he didn't notice was that 10,000 people sang their hearts out, and 10,000 people were silent.

Last Saturday in Montreal, the arena was filled with fans in red-and-white Canada jerseys. The NHL and the NHL Players' Association, which had organized the event, did what organizers do. They asked the fans to be respectful of both teams during the anthems. The fans decided not to be managed. They booed "The Star-Spangled Banner" loudly. They were not booing the American players. They were booing Donald Trump. Why shouldn't he know how they felt? Why shouldn't Americans know? How else would they know?

Five nights later in Boston, at the final game, the fans booed "O Canada," but not very loudly.

The game was a classic. The two best teams in the world: Canada, the heart and soul, conscience and bedrock of the game; the U.S., in its development and growth, the great story in hockey in the past thirty years. Both teams played as well as they'd ever played. Their great stars played like great stars; some other players discovered in themselves something even they didn't know was there. The U.S. could've won. The team was good enough to win. Canada won because of Connor McDavid, Nathan MacKinnon, and Sidney Crosby—and for the same reason Canada won against the Soviets in 1972.

Everybody, every country, has something inside them that is fundamental. That matters so much that it's not negotiable. That's deeply, deeply personal. Something that, if threatened, you'd do anything to protect, and keep on doing it until it's done, even if it seems to others to make no sense. Even if it seems stupid. This is how wars start.

For Panama, some things are fundamental. For Denmark, China, Russia, Germany, Ukraine, Canada—for everyone—it's the same. And when you get pushed too much, too far, you rediscover what that fundamental is. Poke the bear and you find out there's more in the bear than you know, than even the bear knows.

For Canada and these other countries, you don't poke back against Donald Trump. You don't troll a troll. You look into yourselves and find again what makes you special, why you matter, to yourselves, to the world, and knowing that, knowing that that is you, with that as your pride and backbone, you fight back.

The U.S. has its own fights. It faces these same questions. What is fundamental to America? "Greatness"? Maybe. But greatness depends on the needs of a country and the needs of the world at a particular moment and time, and being great in the ways that are needed. These next four years will not be easy for anyone—and they will be perhaps especially difficult for the United States.

As for the 51st state crap, knock it off. It's beneath you.

For Donald Trump, everything is a transaction. You look to make a deal, you push and shove, scratch and claw—you do whatever it takes. And if that doesn't work, you do some more, until at some point you walk away and make another deal. It's just business.

Only, some things aren't business. Every so often, Canadians are defiantly not-American. They will need to be much more than that in the next four years. Canadians will need to be defiantly Canadian. Canada won in 1972 and again last week because winning was about more than business. It was personal.

ELAMIN ABDELMAHMOUD is an award-winning culture writer and host of CBC's *Commotion*. His work has appeared in the *Globe and Mail*, *Maclean's*, *Rolling Stone*, and others. He is the author of *Son of Elsewhere: A Memoir in Pieces*, a number one national bestseller, a Globe 100 book, and a *New York Times* notable book.

MARGARET ATWOOD is the author of more than fifty books of fiction, poetry, and critical essays. Her novels include *Cat's Eye*, *The Robber Bride*, *Alias Grace*, *The Blind Assassin*, and the MaddAddam trilogy. Her 1985 classic, *The Handmaid's Tale*, was followed in 2019 by a sequel, *The Testaments*, which was a global number one bestseller and won the Booker Prize. In 2020 she published *Dearly*, her first collection of poetry in a decade, followed in 2022 by *Burning Questions*, a selection of essays (2004–2021). Her most recent collection of short stories, *Old Babes in the Wood*, was published in March 2023. In October 2024, *Paper Boat*, a collection of new and selected poems (1961–2023), was published. Atwood has won numerous awards, including the Arthur C. Clarke Award for Imagination in Service to Society, the Franz Kafka Prize, the Peace Prize of the German Book Trade, the PEN Center USA Lifetime Achievement

Award, and the Dayton Literary Peace Prize. In 2019 she was made a member of the Order of the Companions of Honour for services to literature. She has also worked as a cartoonist, illustrator, librettist, playwright, and puppeteer. She lives in Toronto.

JAY BARUCHEL is from Montreal and lives in Toronto.

JEANNE BEKER is a Canadian journalist, media personality, and fashion icon. Her memoir, *Heart on My Sleeve* (2024), was released through Simon & Schuster Canada to critical acclaim. With a touching forward by Linda Evangelista, Beker delivers uplifting reflections that walk us through a wardrobe of memory, one article of clothing at a time. Over the years, Beker has acted as an arts reporter for CBC Radio, a news anchor on CHUM Radio, a co-host of *The NewMusic*, a founding member of MuchMusic, and the emblematic host of *Fashion Television* for twenty-seven years. Beker is also a seasoned newspaper columnist for several publications and has authored six books. A frequent keynote speaker and television guest, she currently hosts the series *Style Matters* on The Shopping Channel. Beker was named to the Order of Canada in 2014 and received a star on Canada's Walk of Fame in 2016.

Author and musician **DAVE BIDINI** is the only person to have been nominated for a Gemini, Genie, and Juno as well CBC's *Canada Reads*. A founding member of Rheostatics and member of Bidiniband, he has written thirteen books, including *On a Cold Road*, *Tropic of Hockey*, *Around the World in 57½ Gigs*, and *Home and Away*. He has made two

Gemini Award–nominated documentaries, and his play *The Five Hole Stories* was staged by One Yellow Rabbit Performance Theatre, touring the country in 2008. His third book, *Baseballissimo*, is being developed for the screen by Jay Baruchel, and in 2010 he won his third National Magazine Award, for "Travels in Narnia," followed by Calgary Wordfest's Anne Green Award for artistic audacity. In 2014, he was nominated for a Toronto Arts Award, and in 2017 he launched *West End Phoenix*, Canada's newest broadsheet newspaper. *Midnight Light: A Personal Journey to the North* is his latest book, and in 2023 he co-directed the CBC series *Summit '72*.

MÉLISSA BULL is a writer, editor, and translator based in Montreal. She has published a collection of poetry, *Rue*, a collection of short stories, *The Knockoff Eclipse*, and has translated such works as Nelly Arcan's *Burqa of Skin*, Marie-Sissi Labrèche's *Borderline*, and Valérie Lefebvre-Faucher's *Jenny, Eleanor, and Laura, et al.: This Is Not a Book About Marx*. Her translation of Maxime Raymond Bock's novel *Morel* was a finalist for the 2024 Governor General's Award.

IVAN COYOTE is a writer and storyteller. Born and raised in Whitehorse, Yukon, they are the author of thirteen books, and the creator of four films, six stage shows, and three albums that combine storytelling with music. Coyote's books have won the ReLit Award, been named a Stonewall Honor Book, been longlisted for *Canada Reads*, and been shortlisted for the Hilary Weston Prize for non-fiction, and the Governor General's Award for non-fiction twice. In 2017 Ivan was given an Honorary Doctor of Laws from Simon Fraser University, and in 2023 they received the first Honorary Doctor of Arts ever bestowed on anyone by Yukon University. Coyote's stories grapple with the complex and intensely personal topics of gender identity, family, class, and queer liberation, but always with a generous heart and a quick wit. Ivan's thirteenth book, *Care Of*, was released in June 2021 by McClelland & Stewart, and their new one-person show, *Playlist*, premiered in February 2024. Coyote currently serves as a Specialist in Creative Engagement and Expression at Yukon University.

KEN DRYDEN was a goalie for the Montreal Canadiens in the 1970s, during which time the team won six Stanley Cups. He also played for Team Canada in the 1972 Summit Series. He has been inducted into the Hockey Hall of Fame and Canada's Sports Hall of Fame. He is a former federal member of parliament and cabinet minister, and is the author of multiple books, including *The Game*, *Home Game* (with Roy MacGregor), *Game Change*, and most recently, *The Series*. He and his wife, Lynda, live in Toronto and have two children and four grandchildren.

With eighteen feature films and related projects, **ATOM EGOYAN** has won numerous awards including five prizes at the Cannes Film Festival—the Grand Prix, International Critics' Awards, and Ecumenical Jury Prizes—two Academy Award nominations, twenty-five Genie Awards (now Canadian Screen Awards)—including three Best Film Awards—as well as prizes from the National Board of Review and an award for Best International Adaptation at the Frankfurt Book Fair. Egoyan has been recognized for his critically acclaimed opera productions and was honoured with a 2016 Opera Canada

Award (Rubie) for Film and Stage Direction. *Seven Veils*, Egoyan's most recent film, had its world premiere at the Toronto International Film Festival, 2023, before its international premiere at the Berlin Film Festival, and was screened at the opening night gala at the Yerevan International Film Festival in Armenia in the summer of 2024. *Donation*, an original production written and directed by Egoyan and starring Arsinée Khanjian, was performed in repertory at the Maxim Gorki Theater, Berlin, in spring 2025. It will be remounted later the same year, along with his production of *Jenůfa* by Opéra de Montréal, at Place des Arts. Egoyan is a Companion of the Order of Canada and has received the Governor General's Performing Arts Award.

OMAR EL AKKAD is a writer based near Portland, Oregon. He is the author of two novels, *American War* and *What Strange Paradise*. His books have been translated into more than a dozen languages. His first book of non-fiction, *One Day, Everyone Will Have Always Been Against This*, was an instant *New York Times* bestseller.

CATHERINE HERNANDEZ (she/her) is an award-winning author and screenwriter. She is a proud queer woman who is of Filipino, Spanish, Chinese, and Indian descent, and married into the Navajo Nation. Her first novel, *Scarborough*, won the Jim Wong-Chu Award for the unpublished manuscript and was a finalist for several awards including *Canada Reads* 2022. Its film adaptation was produced by Compy Films and penned by Catherine herself. It won eight Canadian Screen Awards including Best Picture and Best Adapted Screenplay. Her second novel, *Crosshairs*, was shortlisted for the Toronto Book Award and made several best-of lists of 2020. Her most recent books, *The Story of Us* and *Behind You*, were instant national bestsellers. Before *Behind You* hit the shelves, it was optioned by Conquering Lion Pictures to become a feature film, with Catherine writing the screenplay. *Behind You* was longlisted for the Dublin Literary Award. She is working on several TV and film projects, including showrunning CBC Gem/Apartment 11/ Avenida Productions' *The Unstoppable Jenny Garcia*.

JILLIAN HORTON is the author of *We Are All Perfectly Fine: A Memoir of Love, Medicine and Healing*. It won the 2022 Edna Staebler Award for creative non-fiction and is currently being adapted for television. She is a regular contributor to the *Globe and Mail*, the *Los Angeles Times*, and other high-impact print media, where she writes about subjects ranging from medicine to culture and politics. She is an associate professor in the Department of Internal Medicine at the University of Manitoba.

LESLIE HURTIG was born into a house of books and has worked in a range of senior positions across the Canadian literary landscape for the last thirty years. She is the artistic director of the internationally acclaimed literary festival the Vancouver Writers Fest.

JESSICA JOHNSON was born in Saskatoon and has lived in Montreal, Toronto, and Vancouver. An award-winning magazine writer and editor, she has published essays, columns, and features in *The Walrus*, the *Globe and Mail*, the *New Republic*, and many other publications across North America.

From 2009 to 2016, she was the head copywriter behind the international rebranding of Hudson's Bay, and in 2017 became the first woman to edit *The Walrus*, Canada's leading general interest magazine, a role she held for almost six years. In 2025, she released "What Should the CBC Be?"—the results of a two-year national research project on public media in Canada for McGill University's Centre for Media, Technology, and Democracy. Jessica lives in Toronto and Ottawa.

MARGARET LAURENCE (1926–1987) was a Canadian writer born in Neepawa, Manitoba. After graduating from Winnipeg's United College in 1947, she worked as a reporter before living in Africa from 1950 to 1957, where she began writing fiction inspired by her experiences. Returning to Canada, she published works set in Ghana and later moved to England, writing five novels about the fictional town of Manawaka, based on her hometown. Settling in Ontario in 1974, she continued writing fiction, essays, and children's books, earning two Governor General's Awards and numerous honours.

JEN SOOKFONG LEE was born and raised in Vancouver's East Side, and she now lives with her son in North Burnaby. Her most recent horror novel, *The Hunger We Pass Down*, explores family secrets and the ghosts we can never outrun. Her memoir *Superfan: How Pop Culture Broke My Heart* was a finalist for the 2024 Forest of Reading Evergreen Book Award and the City of Vancouver Book Award, named a best book of 2023 by the *Globe and Mail* and Apple Books Canada, and was a *TODAY Show* Recommended Read. She is also the author of *The Conjoined*, nominated for the International

Dublin Literary Award and a finalist for the Ethel Wilson Fiction Prize; *The Better Mother*, a finalist for the City of Vancouver Book Award; *The End of East*; *The Shadow List*; and *Finding Home*. Jen acquires and edits for ECW Press.

CATHERINE LEROUX is a Quebec novelist born in 1979. Her novel *The Party Wall* (*Le mur mitoyen*) was nominated for the 2016 Giller Prize. *The Future* (*L'avenir*) won the 2024 edition of *Canada Reads*. Her latest work, *Peuple de verre*, a speculative fiction about the housing crisis, will be published in English in 2026 by Simon & Schuster. She lives in Montreal with her two children.

CANISIA LUBRIN was born in Saint Lucia. Living in the territories of the Gunshot Treaty of 1792, she is the author of *Voodoo Hypothesis*, *The Dyzgraph*ˣ*st*, *Code Noir*, and *The World After Rain*. Her numerous honours include a Windham–Campbell Prize for poetry, OCM Bocas Prize for Caribbean Literature, Griffin Poetry Prize, Carol Shields Prize for Fiction, and Danuta Gleed Literary Award. She teaches and coordinates the creative writing MFA at the University of Guelph and is the poetry editor at McClelland & Stewart.

ANN-MARIE MACDONALD is a novelist, playwright, actor, broadcast host, recreational hockey player, and proud Canadian. She was born on a NATO base in the former West Germany to a Lebanese Canadian mother and a Scottish Canadian father, both of whom hailed from Cape Breton Island/Unama'ki. She grew up on the move as a Royal Canadian Air Force kid. Her writing for the stage includes the plays

Goodnight Desdemona (Good Morning Juliet), *Belle Moral: A Natural History*, and *Hamlet-911*; the libretto for the chamber opera *Nigredo Hotel*; and the book and lyrics for the musical comedy *Anything That Moves*. Her novels are *Fall on Your Knees*, *The Way the Crow Flies*, *Adult Onset*, and *Fayne*. She has performed on stages across Canada and in numerous TV series, including *Due South*, *The L Word*, and *Slings & Arrows*, as well as feature films including *Better Than Chocolate* and *I've Heard the Mermaids Singing*. Her written work has been honoured with awards including the Commonwealth Prize, the Chalmers, the Governor General's, the Quebec Writers' Federation, the Dora Mavor Moore, the John Drainie, the Gascon-Thomas, the Canadian Authors Association, and the Canadian Booksellers Association; and, as a screen actor, she has been recognized with a Gemini Award. Most of all, as a veteran of the collaborative arts, Ann-Marie is honoured by opportunities like this anthology. In 2019 she was made an Officer of the Order of Canada in recognition of her contribution to the arts and to LGBTQ2SI+ rights. She now lives in Toronto with her wife, theatre director Alisa Palmer, with whom she has two children.

PETER MANSBRIDGE is best known for his five decades of work at the CBC, where he was chief correspondent for CBC News and anchor of *The National* for thirty years. He has won dozens of awards for outstanding journalism, has fourteen honorary doctorates from universities in Canada and the United States, and received Canada's highest civilian honour, the Order of Canada, in 2008. He is the former two-term chancellor of Mount Allison University, now its chancellor emeritus, a distinguished fellow at the Munk School of Global Affairs at the University of Toronto, and is a member of numerous boards and committees. Peter believes strongly in the future of Canadian journalism and has personally funded major new programs at three different Canadian universities: King's University College, Carleton University, and the University of British Columbia. Peter is involved with several projects and initiatives alongside his charitable work. He is the president of Manscorp Media Services, where his work includes documentary film production. In addition, he hosts one of Canada's leading political podcasts, *The Bridge*, and writes the weekly newsletter *The Buzz* for National Newswatch. Peter is also the author of four national bestsellers: *One on One* (2009), *Extraordinary Canadians* (2020), *Off the Record* (2021), and *How Canada Works* (2023).

DAVID MOSCROP is a political columnist, commentator, and author of *Too Dumb for Democracy?: Why We Make Bad Political Decisions and How We Can Make Better Ones*. He holds a PhD in political science from the University of British Columbia, where he studied the psychology of democratic deliberation. He lives in Ottawa.

FARLEY MOWAT (1921–2014) was born in Belleville, Ontario. Following his service in World War II (1940–1945), he began his writing career in 1949 after two years in the Arctic, and travelled extensively across Canada and beyond, including Siberia. Author of forty-two books published in over fifty languages and sixty countries, Mowat's notable works include *People of the Deer*, *Never Cry Wolf*, and *Virunga*. His stories and articles appeared in major magazines.

Toronto-born, Berkeley, California–based writer and musician **PAUL MYERS** communicates popular culture for a living. He is the author of the recent biography *John Candy: A Life in Comedy*, and critically acclaimed previous works *Kids in the Hall: One Dumb Guy*; *A Wizard, A True Star: Todd Rundgren in the Studio*; *It Ain't Easy: Long John Baldry and the Birth of the British Blues*; and *Barenaked Ladies: Public Stunts, Private Stories*. Paul was an executive producer on the 2023 Canadian Screen Award–winning, two-part documentary series *Kids in the Hall: Comedy Punks,* and is the host of the weekly *Record Store Day Podcast.*

CAROL OFF is an author and broadcaster. She is the former co-host of CBC's radio program *As It Happens*, where she conducted more than 25,000 interviews over fifteen years. Before that, Carol spent three decades as a field reporter, covering events in Canada and around the world while producing news and current affairs for CBC radio and television. She is the author of five award-winning and bestselling books, most recently *At a Loss for Words: Conversations in an Age of Rage*.

TOM POWER is the award-winning host of *Q* on CBC Radio One, where his thoughtful and captivating interview style has drawn international acclaim. Since taking over *Q* in 2016, Tom's ability to blend depth with humour has earned him multiple accolades, including gold medals for best interview at the New York Festivals for conversations with Michael J. Fox (2021), Bono (2022), and Mick Jagger (2023). A native of St. John's, Newfoundland, Tom began his broadcasting career at twenty-one, becoming the youngest national radio host in CBC history with *Deep Roots*. He later moved to Toronto to host *Radio 2 Morning*, before stepping into his current role on *Q*. His work has extended beyond radio to include the national TV show *What're You At?*, where he connected with Canadians during the early days of the pandemic. In addition to his broadcasting career, Tom is a co-founder of The Dardanelles, a critically acclaimed band that has played a vital role in the revival of traditional Newfoundland music. The band's energetic performances and dedication to bringing obscure folk tunes to modern audiences have made them a cornerstone in Newfoundland's musical history. Whether behind the mic or on stage, Tom brings his signature warmth and curiosity to everything he does—and when he's not working, he can often be found in pool halls across Canada, trying (and failing) to improve his snooker game.

IAIN REID is a screenwriter and *New York Times* bestselling author of five books, including two works of nonfiction. His debut novel *I'm Thinking of Ending Things* was adapted for Netflix by Oscar-winner Charlie Kaufman. His work has been nominated for various awards including the Governor General's Literary Award and Shirley Jackson Award. His books have been translated into more than twenty languages.

MORDECAI RICHLER (1931–2001) was a celebrated Canadian novelist, journalist, screenwriter, and editor born and raised in Montreal's working-class Jewish neighbourhood. After studying at Sir George Williams College, he lived in London from 1954 until returning to Montreal in 1972. Richler's work often depicted Montreal and Canada, blending satire, humour, and critical insight. He received numerous honours, including the Giller Prize and two Governor General's Awards.

DAVID A. ROBERTSON is a two-time Governor General's Literary Award winner and has won the TD Canadian Children's Literature Award and the Writers' Union of Canada Freedom to Read Award. He has received several other accolades for his work as a writer for children and adults, podcaster, public speaker, and social advocate. He has been honoured with a Doctor of Letters from the University of Manitoba, and a Doctor of Laws from the University of Lethbridge. He is a member of Norway House Cree Nation and lives in Winnipeg.

NIIGAAN SINCLAIR is Anishinaabe from Peguis First Nation. He is an award-winning writer, editor, and professor of Indigenous studies at the University of Manitoba, whose first book, *Wînipêk: Visions of Canada from an Indigenous Centre* (McClelland & Stewart, 2024), was a national bestseller that won the 2024 Governor General Award for Non-fiction.

JESSE WENTE is a husband and father, as well as an award-winning writer and speaker. Born and raised in Toronto, his family comes from Chicago and Genaabaajing Anishinaabek, and he is an off-reserve member of the Serpent River First Nation. Jesse is best known for more than two decades spent as a columnist for CBC Radio's *Metro Morning*. Jesse spent a decade with the Toronto International Film Festival as a curator, including leading the film and gallery programming at the

TIFF Lightbox. In 2018, Jesse was named founding director of the Indigenous Screen Office, and in summer 2020 he was appointed chair of the Canada Council for the Arts. His award-winning first book, *Unreconciled: Family, Truth, and Indigenous Resistance*, was a national bestseller. Jesse was recently named the Storyteller-in-Residence at Toronto Metropolitan University. His first children's book, *Danger Eagle*, is being published by Tundra Books.